The Principles of Business

The Principles of Business

Understanding What Makes a Business
Successful and Valuable to Society

Dave DeRose

THE PRINCIPLES OF BUSINESS
UNDERSTANDING WHAT MAKES A BUSINESS
SUCCESSFUL AND VALUABLE TO SOCIETY

iUniverse books may be ordered through booksellers or by contacting:

iUniverse
1663 Liberty Drive
Bloomington, IN 47403
www.iuniverse.com
1-800-Authors (1-800-288-4677)

Because of the dynamic nature of the Internet, any web addresses or links contained in this book may have changed since publication and may no longer be valid. The views expressed in this work are solely those of the author and do not necessarily reflect the views of the publisher, and the publisher hereby disclaims any responsibility for them.

Any people depicted in stock imagery provided by Getty Images are models, and such images are being used for illustrative purposes only.
Certain stock imagery © Getty Images.

ISBN: 978-1-5320-8692-2 (sc)
ISBN: 978-1-5320-8693-9 (hc)
ISBN: 978-1-5320-8694-6 (e)

Library of Congress Control Number: 2020901694

Print information available on the last page.

iUniverse rev. date: 01/27/2020

Contents

Introduction

My thirty years of being involved in business endeavors have made one thing very apparent to me: everyone wants the freedom to be in business, and few really understand the dedication and effort it takes to be successful. While I was in the plumbing and HVAC business, my theory applies to any business. These are thoughts and experiences I have had over the last thirty years. Some are from personal experiences, and others are from observations, but for me all are pure gold in value.

You may start a business and not find your heart or mind for several years, but I hope these chapters will help you find them, as that will be financially and personally rewarding to you on the journey.

I graduated high school in 1973, and my father had always told me to go to college and get a nice white-collar office job. After looking around in my junior year, I told him I wanted to be a plumber and work with my hands and not be confined to an office. So I went to work for a union plumbing shop as the shop boy and general helper, and as soon as the opportunity to apply for an apprenticeship in plumbing and pipe fitting came up, I applied.

My father taught in the apprentice program, and while you would think that would put me high on the entrance list, it did not. About two years after being put on that list, I started an apprenticeship at a coal-fired plant 170 miles from my hometown. My father, a plumber, was not happy about my being a pipe fitter, but I tried to learn all I could. I became a journeyman pipe fitter, passed a journeyman Colorado plumber's exam on the first try, and became an instructor in the apprenticeship program, like my father, teaching trade math, science, and hydronic heating and cooling.

I worked at this for several years, and then, after becoming a father myself, my wife wanted a divorce. I could not leave my son, so although I could have left and made great money and traveled the country, I stayed in this small town and went to work for a small contractor for a short time. Then I worked for another small shop, which consisted of the owner, a sheet metal worker, and myself. After working for this company for three years and watching how the owner ran the business, I was asked to take a 30 percent cut in pay around the time Chrysler was taking a dollar-per-hour cut and Lee Iacocca was saving that company. I did not know what to do and considered moving to a big city, but then the opportunity to start my own business presented itself.

I had a master plumber's license, I carried the local mechanical contractor's license for this small company, and all I needed were an insurance policy and a pickup truck. A friend had moved to the town in which I grew up and wanted to sell me all his HVAC/refrigeration customers in our small town, so I made the deal on October 1, 1988. I started a new business and hit the ground running.

While I was a union steward on the power plant and also a foreman and had installed a job for Johnson Controls (which is what I really loved to do), I now was a one-man plumbing, heating, and refrigeration contractor. I did it all, and although those days were at times difficult, they were rewarding. Our town was in a big recession, and many days I winterized houses that were bank owned so they would not freeze and be damaged. I fixed everything you could imagine. Two years later, in 1990, I installed my first real contract job. I took all my friends to lunch at the local Village Inn to celebrate my first big contract. (One piece of advice: wait until you are done with that job to see if you made any money before you buy lunch.) I installed boilers and toilets, plumbed hair salons, fixed walk-in freezers, and grew into a company that employed twelve or more and produced around $1.8 million to $2 million per year in a town of about ten thousand people.

It has been a great ride, but there have been issues I hope to help you avoid as you try to grow or refine the business you already have. Here are some things we will talk about that I learned the hard way.

I recommend you find a really good accountant who understands taxes and how they relate to you and your business and can advise you on how to operate. My accountant helped me create a college fund that fully paid for my son's college and left him with $20,000 in the bank. We also bought him a drum set, a new guitar, and a new pickup truck, all while paying for his college. He got a free education, and he has used it to create a graphic design company and is doing well.

I recommend you have some mentors who keep you honest and also help you think through things. Sometimes they can be a supplier, like Bill Olsen was to me, or a former employer, like Bud Moriarty, or even a customer who operates a chain of restaurants. I used to tell him my labor costs were in line but my food costs were out of control. All of these people taught me many things that made my business successful.

Make sure your spouse and family are never hurt by your business. You will work long hours in the beginning, but you still need to be a great spouse and parent. Never let your business take your home. In other words, in times of trouble, do not finance your home to bail out your business. Make sure you can keep a roof over your head.

A good banker who understands business and is not there just to make a loan fee or interest, who thinks of your best interests and gives good advice, will be key to your success. You may need to borrow money, but make sure this is for a profitable reason and not just a personal desire.

In the following chapters, I will cover more of these subjects in depth, but right now I want to give you a brief look at where I came from and what I have experienced.

Never let the success of your business make you a different person. Do not let it change your desire to be generous or a mentor. Do not let it make you a selfish, miserable individual. Basically keep centered in your life. If someone had told me that I would be anything other than a really good plumber and pipe fitter when I entered the trade, I would have called them crazy. My trade consisted of anything that had pipe to it. I did not have a goal of being in business for myself, although I think all people wonder and dream about what that might be like. I never would have thought I would have the opportunity to be on the founding board of a Boys and Girls Club or on the board of directors of a bank. Owning commercial real estate was not something I set out to do, but I own quite a lot at this time. One of my mentors, the author of a book called *Rich Dad Poor Dad*, taught me about that.

Remain hungry for knowledge, and exercise wisdom, which is the proper use of the knowledge you have attained and does not require gray hair (although I have a lot of that). Cultivate relationships with suppliers and contractor friends who are like minded and not in your area. These relationships are very rewarding, and you will find that you are not alone when you think you are.

These are some of my recommendations, and I hope to expand on all of them. I tried to write this book in an interesting and easy-to-read way, and my goal is to inspire you to "be all you can be" and more. That is a great quotation from the US Army, but it applies more to your efforts and your desires than it does to whom you are enlisted with.

Good luck, and Godspeed.

The Desires of Your Heart

Scripture states that "out of the abundance of the heart the mouth speaks." Jesus said that to a group of Pharisees after calling them vipers. I believe that whatever we read that came from Jesus is not just about the time but a statement of fact. Jesus was condemning this group for their language and their deeds. Understanding how you think and how that leads to your actions is important for your future and will shelter you from bad decisions and actions that Jesus called out in the Pharisees.

What does your heart desire? What are you willing to work for? You do not have to be a dyed-in-the-wool, churchgoing, bible-thumping Christian to make these words true. I believe they are true for the entire universe. We all have desires and things we enjoy, and for each person those may be different.

I have several friends who are really interested in hunting, horses, rodeo, baseball, and even golf. I have to admit I am not interested in any of those things. Some of those same folks do not care about classic cars or football, like I do. The same is true for someone's ability to be in business or to handle the daily rigors and stress of their position.

While a member of our city council in addition to six years as mayor, I heard from many folks that they could not stand politics and could never do what I was doing. I can tell you it is all what you make of it. I presume if I dedicated myself to the study of the game of golf, like I did politics, I would have a respectable handicap and enjoy the game. My game is a clear indicator that I did not study or practice that sport.

You must do some soul-searching to ensure that you really want to be in business. You may already be there and feel trapped, or you may already be there and not care about how it goes. Not only is that damaging to you, but it is damaging to your family, employees, and customers as well. I have witnessed businesses, which were being run by an individual who really did not want to be there, sell to someone who did. The same business that was a thorn in the side of the first owner became a blessing to the second.

I think attitude and desires make the difference in this reality, and a true accounting of both will pay dividends even if you do not go into business for yourself. We are taught to "count the cost" of any activity we encounter, and that is really what we are saying.

A good example is the individuals who start a business and immediately begin to buy new vehicles and toys. They are making so much money and never consider the cost to themselves or the business that will eventually, if run appropriately, become a cash cow and provide more than they could ever have imagined. This may take several years of hard work, but it is worth it to endure, as it will pay great dividends if you do. The owner who immediately buys new items did not "count the cost" and will probably be in trouble with the bank.

This type of activity is indicated by the owner who states, "We are a small business and cannot afford to pay more than [fill in the blank], and we cannot pay for [fill in the blank]." That same person will charge for service that everyone else does but wants to hoard as much as they can since they are extending themselves too far. Usually they fail, and then it is the fault of any number of other folks, from the bank to employees to their customers. I heard it said once that when we point a finger at someone, there are three pointing back at us, and I think that is a good thing to monitor before we begin to lay blame.

I am not saying that there are not times things happen beyond our control that have negative or even life-threatening effects on our business, but I think studies will show that most business failures are caused by the folks in control and not the outside influences.

If you genuinely want to build a business that will be a part of your community and you want to become a leader in your industry, then you will approach the business differently. You will build for the long haul and not to benefit from the immediate profit. You will desire to build the lives of your employees into something better than they have and not to use their labor just for your gain. I have said many times that a business should profit from the sweat of the employees but not the blood of them.

That being said, while some folks may not work out as members of your team and leave either by your choice or theirs, you need to examine why they were not productive in your employ. Maybe they were never productive for anyone, but I know folks who were very profitable to me at one time or another who then took a path of self-destruction and caused more problems and made more mistakes than any business can allow. These were not folks who needed more training or were unable to work in the system. Rather, they decided to push the envelope and see how far we would allow them to get out of line.

The last paragraph aside, are your desires to build something born from a good place, or are you driven by greed and selfishness? Look at your heart, and be honest with yourself. You will reap what you sow, and that is not always what you want to happen.

I have spent twenty-seven years in business, but I did not intend to be a self-employed business owner. Upon my graduation from Grand Junction High School, I entered the plumbing and heating trade and eventually served an apprenticeship with the local plumbers and pipe fitters union and even taught classes in the apprenticeship program after becoming a journeyman. After several years, I took the master plumbers exam for Colorado and just held that in reserve.

By this time I was sure I was meant to be some great company's top mechanic and would be paid for it well and have a great life. All of that changed in 1988, when the company I was working for decided they had a cash flow problem and needed to reduce my salary. The 25–30 percent reduction created a new salary of $10.60 per hour. I decided I had to stay in Craig, Colorado, and raise my eight-year-old son. The only option I could see was to become a one-man plumbing shop and try to make a better life for us.

There was a time when I thought I would turn out as a journeyman, and my father (a seasoned plumber in Grand Junction), who had been a go-to service plumber for years, would pass the master's test, and we would start a business that would take Grand Junction by storm. I think all young men have dreams like that, but I quickly decided I was much better served by working for someone else at a fair wage and, as I said, be a top mechanic for them.

By the time I was presented with the idea of being in business for myself, my father had retired, and I was faced with either moving, just enduring the reduced wages, or making a change. I made the latter choice, with some help from a friend who wanted to sell his clients in Craig, as he had moved to Grand Junction and started a new client list there. We struck a deal, and I am proud to say I still consider Bill a great friend to this day, although we really do not see enough of each other.

The change in my life was dramatic, and I began to bid on work and perform service calls, while wondering how long I could make this last. I bought my first 1988 Chevrolet in 1990, after being in business for two years, and took out a loan at the local bank. I remember thinking that now I had to keep it going, as I could not just quit if I had a loan. Now that seems oddly humorous.

For the next twenty-five years I kept at it and bought many other trucks, buildings, and tools, not to mention that I took many trips based on how much I traveled to (and bought from) suppliers. I eventually met a wonderful woman ("Linda") who changed my life and gave me the ability to concentrate on the business and not worry about the books.

I grossed $27,000 in my first three months in business, and in 1989 our yearly gross was around $125,000. I decided that if I could charge one hundred hours per month of labor at $30 per hour, I could make a living equal to what I was making with my former employer and even pay for all expenses and a $500-per-month bill at the plumbing supply house. The business today rarely spends less than $15,000 to $20,000 per month at our major suppliers to keep the work rolling.

I still did not know what my heart desired, although I was in business, but I knew that I wanted to make a living, and it was apparent to me that I could not do all the work I could land by myself. I originally listened to many other people who tried to convince me that a small business would not provide things like fair wages and benefits. It was easy to adopt that attitude. Most small-business owners in our small town believed that and did not expect any better of themselves or the business climate.

I have always believed that your heart will lead you and show you the right way to do things. I knew I wanted better for myself, my family, and employees. I began to see the possibility when I met Presley, a retired businessman who had moved to Craig with his wife, Patty, and showed us how to take care of our community and children. He was instrumental in starting a Boys and Girls Club, of which I was asked to serve on the founding board. At the time of this writing I am still on that board. He made me read the book *Good to Great,* which confirmed in my heart that we can do things better. It changed my thinking dramatically. I began to look for the right fit for Masterworks and for the city of Craig, as I was serving on the city council at the time and later as mayor. I just knew we could do better.

That Boys and Girls Club, with the addition of a branch in Steamboat Springs in 2009, became the fifth largest club in Colorado after starting in Craig in 2004. Today it serves 50 percent of the youth aged six to about fourteen in both communities with a budget of around $1 million. God really will grant good things to those who wait and listen. At the same time, Masterworks was making great strides. We were over $1 million in gross revenue per year, with our best year bringing about $2.4 million. We had a 401(k) plan and health insurance for the families of our employees and good trucks to drive home for all our main technicians and installers. All the trucks were the same color. We had created a signature in our area.

What are the desires of your heart? As you think about starting, buying, or operating a business, this is a question you must answer. I do not have a formula or even understand the complete turn of events that put me in this position, but some days when I think of my life, now that I am sixty-four and have sold the company, I am thankful for what I have learned and experienced. I cannot imagine life any different from what it has been.

The trials and rewards are worth the results, or, as some might say, "the juice is really worth the squeeze." While there have been many things I would have never wanted to experience, it is now easy to see that they were a necessary part of how I became who I am today. I get excited when I see young business owners take on a challenge and begin to see the positive results of their efforts. It reminds me of what Bud Moriarty said to me when I visited his business in Denver and told him I was going into business myself. "Dave, I wish I was your age and starting all over with you, as it is an exciting time, and you will make it. I know." Wow! What a compliment! He missed the challenges and wanted to start over with me?

That, I guess, is why I get excited when I see young business owners take on the challenge and begin to make it. When they buy their first new truck or new equipment, I feel like I want to start over with them and help them with the crafting of their future.

No matter the desire of your heart, this is not a get-rich-quick scheme but one that will provide for you and your family. It is one of the most rewarding things you can do. I often say I have been married to one good woman, owned two Corvettes, and owned my high school car twice, and I am ready to go. I really do not have a bucket list beyond that. I do not think I could live without seeing the challenges and rewards other young business owners' faces and offering my help when called upon and even from time to time making sure they get help when they do not know they need it.

I do not think that anyone has a clear picture of what they want in life. I went on a blind date when I was twenty, just before I moved from Grand Junction to Craig. I had a good friend who had met and later married a great gal. I asked them if she had any friends or sisters like her whom I could meet. They did, and I went on one blind date with her. In the middle of that date, she announced that she would have to marry someone either rich or able to build a new house for her, as she did not plan to live in a mobile home or an apartment. I thought that was a little premature and never asked her out again. She did, however, marry a carpenter friend of mine, and he built her a new house, for which I roughed in the plumbing one weekend before we were measured for our tuxedos for the wedding. By the way, I have lived in apartments and mobile homes, and it really did not hurt me.

When I discuss the desires of your heart, I am focused on how the events or your life will affect your personality and your spiritual makeup. Most folks have no idea what their strengths and weaknesses are and have never even thought about it. It is a really good idea to spend some time reflecting on this subject and seeing what you are made of. Many times this is called a SWOT (strengths, weaknesses, opportunities, and threats) exercise. This will come into play throughout your life. How you handle SWOT is written in your personality code.

Have you ever met someone who seems to know the next move no matter what they are doing? And maybe you know a person who is so disorganized that you wonder how they can get out of bed in the morning and find the bathroom to brush their teeth. That is part of who they are. Both of these folks could be siblings raised in the same house with the same parents, attending the same schools at roughly the same time.

Another example is the couple that has their first child who sleeps all night and is always happy and healthy and smiles and coos. Then they have the demon child who is into everything and never sleeps all night and has no desire to smile at anyone, be it Mom and Dad or Grammy or Papa. As they grow up, the first child is never in trouble in school, never makes a fuss, always gets good grades, and is the most polite child in the universe. The demon child is always in trouble, is usually bored and looking for more activity, and is always challenging authority.

These people live in the same house, have the same lineage, go to the same schools, and eat the same food. What is the difference? There are many references in the New Testament to diverse gifts. Some are called out as wisdom or knowledge. Think about how some folks understand numbers and finance, and others understand mechanical things. Think about how you may enjoy hunting and fishing and possibly even golf, but I enjoy football and cars and even some parts of just working. Your makeup will help to determine what you want in life. That does not mean you will be rich beyond your wildest imagination and you will never have a problem. That means that when you are set in motion in the things for which you are built, it is pure bliss.

A good friend always reminds me that polite women never accomplished anything, and I can see in her makeup that she has a focused streak that makes her do the things she does to reach others and better their lives. She wants to help every person she meets and does so quite often. While others may not be on the front lines, they fill a major role in an organization, and without them the group would be as lost as without a leader.

Look at yourself, and conduct your own SWOT analysis, and then make your choices from there. This great country offers freedom to anyone who wants to put forth the effort to change their lives and better themselves. I believe that when you do, and you then attempt to better others as well, that is the real reward that we all seek. I did not know this forty-six years ago, when I graduated high school, but I know now that without the reward of building an organization that helps to change the face of a community, I would have been unfulfilled. It will not happen instantly, as you will have to grow into the role of making a difference, but I promise it is worth the time.

If I had laid out a blueprint of my life in 1973, when I graduated Grand Junction High School and began to learn a trade, I could not have imagined a better outcome. While there were trials to get here, I found the desires of my heart. Make sure they are of good reports and bring positive things to your world and community, and for sure the juice is worth the squeeze.

I encourage you to look at yourself and determine if you want to dedicate the next five to ten years of your life to this business. You may already be working in the trade, but you rarely are on call sixty to seventy hours a week. While the boss for whom you are working may appear to have it easy, walk a mile in his or her shoes and see what it is like.

Another friend who has been in the same plumbing/HVAC business for more years than I have told me that when he sold the business, he went from working sixty hours a week to nothing in less than a month. It was driving him crazy. We have been on many trips together with suppliers, and this change in his and my lives, while it is what we wanted, comes at a shock to us, since we are so accustomed to working that many hours a day.

And while the hours we put in are not always physical or demanding from a production standpoint, the stress we both learned to deal with is something that we grew used to over a period of time. When I started, I wanted to overlook this stress, as I was building a life for myself and my son, but it soon became part of the routine. I went to the office on Sunday and spent six hours on billing, bidding, cleaning, or just planning the next week. I grew to enjoy that and felt I was being lazy if I did not do that. Some choose to work late nights, and some choose to work early mornings. I usually worked from 6:30 a.m. to about 6:00 p.m. at the shop five days a week and then three to five hours on Saturday and six on Sunday. I was comfortable with that and grew into that routine. I do not think I could work forty hours a week and be happy.

If your heart desires these things, then do not say I did not tell you so. If you are not willing to place your business interests only behind God and your family, then I would recommend you not take this step.

If you are not willing to build a business that is the pinnacle of your industry in your area (and maybe even surrounding areas), then please do not mess up the market for those who want to do that. What do I mean by that? Be a leader in your industry, and learn from those who are older and wiser than you. Find a way to afford proper treatment for your employees, and provide them with a career, not just a job. Give them something to be proud of. Hold high standards in all you do, and never allow those to be compromised by lack of attention or laziness on your part or the part of any of your staff. Demand excellence in all you do.

In 1996, we opened a new downtown location, had a big open house, and fed at least one thousand people brisket sandwiches and drinks. We showed off our new location and all we could do. Before this day, I received a potted plant from a competitor who congratulated me on our new location. This guy was one of the oldest Lennox furnace dealers in the United States. I called him up and invited him to lunch, and he came. In the room we set up as a kitchen, he shook my hand in front of three or four folks who were his good friends and loyal customers. They turned up for our open house and congratulated me on my shop and my success. They said he was proud to call me his best competitor. Do things right, work hard, and never take advantage of your customer. This man was a class act, and while he has passed on, I still talk to his brother. His friends and customers agreed with his assessment of my business, and to this day I am as proud of that comment as I was when a former boss told me he wished he was starting over with me because I had the stuff.

Evaluate yourself, and decide. Do you have the stuff it takes to be successful? What do you want out of life? And is this juice worth your squeeze?

Leadership

We discuss leadership in every industry and venue these days. We send our youth to camps, seminars, and classes to make them leaders. It has been my experience that these are often just character development programs, and while I support the development of every individual's character, that is not really leadership. Leading, in reference to owning your own company or being an "elected leader" (those who are elected are not necessarily leaders), is much different than developing your character.

We quote great leaders from our history. One who sticks out to me is Vince Lombardi. He said, "Winning isn't everything; it's the only thing." Often we forget that he was also an advocate to keep your life in this order: God, family, and football. While you may not enjoy football, you can easily replace it with your business.

What gave Vince Lombardi the right to make these statements? You have to look at his life. He was dedicated to God and his church; he was dedicated to his family; and he had played and learned the business and game of football to a much greater level than almost anyone in his time. That gave him the right to be a leader.

Let's look at being a leader in your business. While my experience is in plumbing and heating, any business can be used for this. A true leader is in line with the sign on the desk of President Harry Truman: "The Buck Stops Here." While most people want that to mean all the money stops here, it also means all the responsibility and stress stop here as well. Having worked with many other business owners and managers in my time, I can tell you that the money stopping here is usually all they want to hear about and not the other things that go with that.

Any time you ask an employee to do something, you should be willing and/or able to do it yourself. That gives you the right to be the leader in that task. You have to take the time, even if it hampers your personal fun time, to learn about what you are doing and be aware of what it takes to accomplish the task you are asking your staff to take on or, in some instances, struggle through.

We tend to think that if we can do something, our employees should be able to do it too. We often forget what it was like to be first-time parents. Children do not come out of the womb with the ability to walk or talk or control bodily functions. I remember wanting to play catch with my son when he was born. As my neighbor played catch with his boy down the street, I would look at my son in the crib and try to throw him a little foam football. He never caught it. By the time he was six, however, we played catch every night, and he developed the skills that made this a great experience.

Use the same concept in regard to your new employees. They can talk and walk, and we hope they can control their bodily functions, but they cannot catch every ball you may want to throw at them. You may want them to catch touchdown passes when they have never seen a football before. That is an unrealistic demand many employers often place upon new employees.

Even if you hire a veteran of your industry (and for my industry, let's use a long-term sheet metal mechanic who has worked in the industry for five years), that does not mean they will understand some of the knowledge that you want to impart. Even a veteran football player can go to another team and not prove to be successful there, even though he had been great at the former location.

A leader realizes that all mankind may have been created equal, but the individual journeys have left them with varied experience and performance levels. Take the guy who has been in the plumbing industry for ten years and still does not possess a license in the state in which he is working. What does that say about him?

Over the years in business, I have employed many individuals with varied success, and I learned quickly that everyone was not raised with the same values and decision-making capability that I had. The reason I address this in leadership is to bring to the forefront that issue in your mind. An employee may be struggling to make ends meet, or another employee may seem incapable of stopping a progression of bad choices. Or you, as a businessperson, may not be able to focus on the important issues facing you in the management of all aspects of your business. I am a firm believer that you must decide to be in business not only for the profit but also for the dedication to all the management ideas. Our country will prosper when employers decide to take their roles seriously and manage great businesses.

One of my favorite TV shows is a business show called *The Profit*. In this show an investor and seasoned business owner travel the country and help struggling businesses. It always amazes me that most businesses have the same issues, and they all tend to point to the owners. Some owners refuse to lead and only yell, while others just sit and watch the time go by while the business goes down the tubes. In many cases individuals have been with the company for several years and have chosen to stay because they want to see the business succeed. Without leadership, that eventually fades, and they leave.

Many on this show remind me of experiences I have had with employees and the lack of discipline I have seen. Some of the employees seem to be there only to take advantage of the poor skills of the owner. Trust me that this happens everywhere, and the sooner you realize it and build the skills to deal with it, the better you will be.

Leadership also looks constantly to the future of the company and attempts to improve not just the money they make but the entire operational health of the organization. Do we need to plan for new trucks? Do we need to change some of our shop layout? Do we have the right folks on the bus, and are there drains on our productivity that we should change? These are some of the questions a leader constantly asks and thinks about. You cannot make any change that is not born out of planning, counting the costs for the change, and measuring the outcomes.

In other chapters we'll discuss things like changing direction, building a crew, and capitalization. In my experience as a business owner, an elected official, and board member for nonprofit organizations, I have witnessed the lack of dedication to leadership in all of these situations.

One example is the contractor who wants to grow the business but is unwilling to make the commitment to be organized and productive. The easiest thing to do is to sell more work, but leadership realizes the abilities of any organization. Selling work is not what makes a profit; completing work in a profitable manner does. I am not suggesting that you take a no-growth stance on your business but that you make the commitment to ensuring you are not just selling work and then worrying about the outcome of following through with it. We talk about risk assessment in another chapter, and this is a major portion of your job as a leader.

If you want to grow, make sure you have created the machine that will facilitate that growth. Do you have the manpower? Do you need more equipment, such as trucks and tools? What will this cost? Can you grow that to a profit?

Making the decision to buy a scissor lift does not ensure you will profit from that purchase. I later outline my purchase of a Nytech layout table and what that has done for us, but I did not buy one until I was sure it would pay dividends to my operation.

To be a leader, you must constantly adjust your plan and realize when you have reached a good spot in your business. You may want to grow your gross, but that is only vanity, as gross revenues mean nothing but the ability to brag that you are billing X amount per month or year. Volume is vanity, profit is sanity, and the P&L is fact. Many companies have operated well and then left the core profit centers to embark on new frontiers, and those normally do not pan out well. Thoughtful, controlled growth is always more profitable than selling work.

When I was first elected to office, I wanted to make our community a better place in which to live. One issue we encountered was the subject of recycling. For a small community, that was a problem. Our solid waste department wanted to enter the roll-off dumpster business, as we had the need for that here and there were no private providers. With the advent of the truck and roll-off business, we were able to set up a recycling depot with three covered roll-off dumpsters and make an agreement with a private company to take the recycled product. Cardboard is, of course, a big item, and with little cost to the consumer or the city, we could collect this item and keep it out of our landfill. We could have taken the stand to have curbside recycling at an enormous cost or just forget it. I believe leaders find the compromise solution that benefits all involved, understanding that it is not always perfect for everyone but utilizing the available resources to make the greatest impact.

As you face problems or issues that only the leader can resolve always seek the solution that provides the best resolve possible. That is true leadership. There also will come a time when you cannot make an impact on a situation with your present resources, so, as a leader, you must choose to wait and reevaluate the next move. While you are waiting, there will always be opportunities to make great changes somewhere else. You may need to make the decision to make the change that is better for all involved with your present situation. This is always a judgment call, and it should not be taken lightly. You must place yourself in the role of making the best call for all situations presented to you. That can mean even the termination of one employee, which will impact your company and the rest of the staff in a positive manner, but it is hard to see the positive side for that employee. In my experience, employees will see change in their lives as well, and the outcome is their responsibility. A change like is often positive for all involved.

My experience with nonprofit organizations is mostly in our local Boys and Girls Club, of which I have served on the board for fourteen years. I was also on the founding board of this organization, as well as served as president of the board. I have been involved since the beginning, so I experienced the issues involved in opening the club, from hiring positions with which we were unfamiliar to raising support and finding locations to operate it. We were faced with everything from completing tasks for the national organization to obtain a charter, to hiring a director who could take us into the future. Adjustments were made through this course, and while there were times I thought this would never work, the club today is standing in two communities, with about 50 percent of the children in both communities between the ages of six and thirteen as members. In this time frame the organization has raised over $1 million a year to fund the work we do, and juvenile contact with law enforcement has dropped. This is not just because of the leadership of the board; the right folks were placed in the organization, and they were managed to see the expectations that need to happen to make the club a viable and productive institution in both communities.

Before we embarked on finding an additional club site, we, as a board, asked ourselves if we would expand if the opportunity presented itself. In 2006, we decided we would, and in 2009, a member of the neighboring community contacted us with volunteers to serve and the money to start a club there. Luck favors the prepared mind, and we were able to take this on. I cannot tell you that all on our board were 100 percent behind this move, but they offered little resistance, and we made the move. Today is the proof of having made the right decision. We reach many children who need the safe place we provide after school, and both communities realize how blessed we are to have this organization in our small towns.

I'm not telling you these stories to pat myself on the back. Rather, I want you to know what to look for as a leader. You must educate yourself and be serious about leading your business or any other organization with which you work. This can be your church or the PTA at your children's school.

To be successful in business, you must be a leader. I have witnessed many who never were and still made a profit. I often think they could have been much better off if they had learned leadership skills. My wife was always my backup in business, making sure all the paperwork T's were crossed and I's were dotted. We often hired a bookkeeper/secretary, and my wife would try to train the new hire as problems arose. I thought she should take two weeks off and spend eighty hours training them so we would know for sure. Her reply was always "I do not have time." I am sure that the eighty hours would have returned eight hundred hours of free time over the course of just two or three years. Leaders never think about the time they have but rather the time they can use to enhance productivity. Think about the easier life the extra time spent may garnered. For me that is time well spent. The cost was negligible.

Leaders operate from a position of truth. John 8:32 says that we will know the truth and it will set us free. Is it true that our world and country are in turmoil? Yes, it is. And there is a great debate today about climate change. While there are great arguments on both sides of this issue, the truth is that we should want to keep our air and water as clean as we possibly can, not only in our backyard but in the entire world. So if we really want to do that, why would we continue to move our manufacturing to a country that has built so many coal-fired power plants with no emissions controls? And we move to shut down all of ours, with the idea that windmills and solar panels will replace them at all costs. How does this help anyone? Would not the better tactic be to use the most efficient production of power and explore safe nuclear and develop the utopian concept we see in *Star Trek* with a never-ending nonpolluting ball of energy that powered spaceships the size of most medium-sized cities across the galaxy? We will not reach that with debate; we will reach that only with leadership and action. Folks on both sides of the debate will have to end the rhetoric and decide to make a change. Use the best knowledge you have now, and work toward dilithium crystals or whatever they had in *Star Trek*.

I gave a tour of a boiler room to a group that wanted to look at the use of green energy. We had just replaced a boiler that was installed in the midseventies with a new condensing and modulating model. We saved them around 30 percent on the energy bill, and that means we reduced the carbon footprint of that facility 30 percent. I told the group that for the price of one windmill, I could reduce the carbon footprint of every commercial building in my town 30 percent, and that would be a greater achievement than one windmill. I relate this to illustrate the point that if leadership is operating from the truth, their good, honest decisions impact the future and make a significant difference.

Another responsibility of leadership is the constant monitoring of all operations. As soon as you rely on another to carry out a task without leadership involved, you have begun to fail as a leader. The size of your organization will dictate how you administer that leadership. If your organization employees more than twelve people, you will have to rely on delegation to make your leadership work. That said, you must be vigilant in overseeing the outcome of the organization.

Let's say you have six crews of ten employees, and each crew is given a supervisor to manage and monitor the production of that crew. You must track each crew and be aware of their progress as they work toward the goals you have set. Leadership keeps a short account of the progress, and that means if progress is not happening on a crew, you find out why and correct it. That may mean different supervisors and even a different crew.

In my experience on large construction sites, many times the individuals least capable of producing were made supervisors. The Peter principle was executed to the fullest. The Peter principle is the concept that everyone will rise one step past where they are effective, and then they will just remain there until they leave of their own accord. In other words, we all know they are not efficient and probably not happy, but we refuse to deal with the mess we made. The Peter principle would cease to influence our outcomes if we just took the time to lead and take that individual back to the level in which they were effective and train them to move up. This is usually tied to compensation. I submit that you would be well served to leave compensation where it is and reduce the individual's responsibility to the point they are successful rather than spend that money and keep the mistakes in play.

Leaders must quickly realize the issue and work to resolve it before it becomes a cancer to the entire organization. That will keep the progress going forward and usually keep employees happier than if nothing was done, which we have a tendency to do.

Leadership puts in place both written and cultural standards. McDonald's is the business leadership example for managing desired success that we should all model. Just like Henry Ford developed a new way to manufacture automobiles, McDonald's developed the way to take high school students part-time and a few full-time adults and produce results that could be replicated in any location with training and discipline. Training and discipline are important and must be always considered together, as training without discipline is nothing more than a social gathering with a central topic. You might as well be going to a play or a movie or even a concert. Unless we become disciples of the information that was introduced in the training and make it a habit, we will not create the difference needed to make the productive change.

I used the term "disciple," which is normally viewed as a religious word, because in reality it means you have adopted a truth and choose to always operate in that truth. Without discipline, no disciples will be made, and little will change. That means that you check the progress of the training and make sure the processes and the information are being used and followed.

Here is a great way to look at this. Have you ever been presented with a child who was constantly making a disruption and the parent continued to scold them and promise a form of discipline but never administer that discipline? The parent says things like "I am going to count to three, and if you are not in line I will _____." Fill in the blank with your own words. When I was young I never got anywhere near three, as I knew there were consequences to my actions.

Business leaders many times make threats like "Turn in your time sheet, or I will withhold your paycheck." We are not going to discuss the legality of that, but the hollow threat will not make any change in the operation of the staff, since they know you will not follow through on any of these threats. One well-placed termination of an individual who refuses to comply will do wonders for this problem.

Be sure your staff knows that you are serious about the consequences you are preaching, and make the changes when needed. I have two nieces who tend to not listen to any adult around until I speak to them, as they know I mean business, and they usually straighten right up. I have spent many hours with them, reading to them and spending time with them, and gained their respect and love. That does not mean I will put up with their insubordination, and no leaders of any organization should put up with it either.

Effective leaders also constantly strive to improve their leadership skills. The use of books and training is important, as well as the fellowship of other leaders in your industry. If you desire to be in business or in charge, then be a leader, and seek every opportunity to improve. It is easy to call yourself a leader, but owning a business or being elected does not make you a leader any more than sleeping in a garage makes you an automobile. Just being parked in a space does not a Cadillac make.

Let's address the normal leadership progression. New leaders are usually enamored with their ability to secure the position, and due to that they tend to make a lot of operational waves. New leaders must take time to learn the structure of the organization to determine how to make the productivity changes needed for success. You may find some individuals who are always moving at a breakneck pace, and those are usually mistaken as your productive team members. Many times they prove to be the most expensive members of your team, as the motion you see may not be hustle but an attempt to keep you guessing. More often they are disorganized and never efficient at their assigned tasks.

You may notice other employees who move at a steady rate that seems slow at first, but upon further investigation it is apparent that they accomplish more in a day than any other staff member you have. Young leaders may make a huge mistake with this observation and impact the team negatively. A slow and deliberate approach is best here. When you see things that require changes, do not be afraid to make them. I often tell new city council members that it will take at least two years on the council to learn where the restrooms are. Upon taking office, newly elected officials do not even know what they do not know. Read that last statement several times, and let it sink in.

When you become a new leader, remember just that—you are a new leader. You do not have the respect or the knowledge to make sweeping changes in the organization. Leadership operates from a position of respect and loyalty. It is up to you, the leader, to earn that; it is not owed to you.

The next step in good leadership progression is productivity. With the respect needed and the use of your gift as a leader, you can make the organization operate at peak performance. While we all like to think we are the best there ever was, every record is meant to be broken. You did not invent the operation or define supreme performance. There always will be someone better than you. Now that you have a good target or course, make the most of the time you have ahead, and be a true leader. Tell the truth, inspire productivity, promote teamwork, and become the most trusted leader you can be to all of your team. Remind yourself that there may be individuals on that team you cannot lead, and move on through that. It is not something to mourn or celebrate; it is just the way things are. This phase can last as long as you want to keep up the good work.

As leaders become complacent or bored in their position, the rest of their organization will follow them. This is a time to consider leaving. Some might think, *My work here is done.* I think that happens eventually to all leaders, but I also know that many times it is an excuse to get out of leadership. The problem with this step is that we do not progress from effectiveness to deciding to make a change. We normally take some time (even years) to get to this next step. Sometimes due to our lack of drive, the decision is made for us. Employers may make the decision for a hired leader, such as a manager or CEO. Customers eventually make the decision for the owner of a business.

Business owners must address their leadership. You cannot take time to *not* be a leader in your organization. You are the coach and quarterback, and there is no taking a play off. If you are in this step of the progression, you owe it to yourself, your customers, and your team to pull out of this nosedive. In 2012, I decided to run for county commissioner. As I thought about that possible new adventure, I took my eye off the ball. My company, while never getting to the point of oblivion, suffered, as the leader (or father of it, if you will) was no longer really interested in the organization. I felt that soon someone else would run this, as I was tired. I wanted to go set the politics of the county on fire with my abilities. I was not elected. While that hurt, I am now glad. I had to come back, take the reins again, and make the necessary changes to keep the company not only alive but profitable.

I took some time off, and I had to work two to three times as hard to recover. This all came in 2009, after the market in our area suffered, and I had struggled through that time without decreasing staff or salaries (with the exception of mine). We still had the same staff, and they worked a full week unless they chose to take off time from work. After three years of that, is it any wonder I was tired and wanted to do something different? It was a difficult but rewarding experience to climb back onto the saddle and ride to victory again.

True leadership is a gift. It is even mentioned in the bible as the gift of government. Those in the New Testament church who possessed this gift were usually chosen to be the deacons, as they had the skills to make the operation run smoothly. You can use the gift to become stronger, just like lifting weights makes your arms or legs stronger. But to exercise this gift, you cannot just accept a position; you must lead.

Once it is time for you to leave, it is the leader's responsibility to make sure the transition is as smooth as possible. Many businesses sell or change hands. Sometimes the transfer is successful, but oftentimes it is not. If you are the departing leader, you must make yourself as available as you can, with the goal to not be there in the future. The new leader must take responsibility for taking as much as possible from the departing leader and making this transition as painless as possible.

When I left my position as mayor, many of the city staff wanted me to run for city council. My term was limited as mayor. I chose to not do that. I felt the new leadership needed to be able to operate without my presence, but I was always available, if needed, to offer any assistance that was within my ability and was requested. I am sure that was the appropriate decision for me and for the city.

I hope this discussion of leadership helps with your journey, but more importantly I hope it wakes up in you the ability to keep all the balls in the air and make a living organization out of your business or the team that you lead. Remember that leadership is a gift that you must exercise to strengthen.

Stinking Thinking

Many have seen the Stuart Smalley skit that *Saturday Night Live* aired in the late nineties. It showcased an individual who obviously was substandard in his emotional state, but he always talked about "stinkin' thinkin'." While it was a funny skit, the phrase still rings true. This type of thinking is what holds back the process that can make you successful.

In other chapters we discuss the books and mentors that will help you to succeed, and we discuss a few relevant situations. We will delve into why we think like we do. One experience I was blessed with in my early career was in the apprenticeship classes. I drove 150 miles twice per month to teach trade math and science at the local plumbers and pipe fitters hall. One Saturday the coordinator had planned for all students and teachers to sit in the meeting hall and watch a film titled *What You Are Is Where You Were When.* It sounds pretty boring, and I am sure most of the students wanted to be in the welding class, making smoke and burning rods, but they had to sit there. This film was presented by a speaker who talked at a very fast rate. We really had to listen to what he had to say. The premise of this presentation was that when we were ten to twelve years old, we decided what was right or wrong, black or white, good or bad.

Think about that. When I was ten, it was 1965. A new car cost around $3,000. A new Corvette cost around $5,000 or $6,000. And a person in my industry earned about $3 to $5 per hour and lived in a house that cost less than $20,000 to purchase. The United States was in the midst of a recovery from the economy of 1958, and things were moving along well. In 1963, JFK was assassinated, and in 1967, Israel started the Six-Day War. TV was a big move in our society, and most churches preached against the depravity of what we saw on *Bonanza* and *The Ed Sullivan Show*. Most of our things were made in the USA, and we all thought items from Japan were cheap junk. A radical who wanted a foreign car drove a VW Beetle. The Beatles were a very popular band, and they had not yet visited the Maharishi. The Beach Boys were still singing about their 409. Most homes had a TV, and many had rabbit ears or an antenna on the roof. Few had cable, with stations from as far away as Chicago and Atlanta. There were race riots in the South, and for the first time we were able to watch as Walter Cronkite showed us our world in color. Captain Kirk and Spock went where no man had gone before.

How do you think my mind was shaped by this? What was happening when you were ten or twelve? The film I watched in my apprenticeship class made me realize some of the reasons I thought like I did and why my Father, a WWII veteran, thought like he did, although we were both in the same trade union and performed the same work. When he was ten, it was 1928. I hope you understand American history enough to know what he lived through.

So when you were 10 or so what was going on in the world and how did that have an effect on your thinking? Only you can say. Take some time to reflect on that.

Now you are an adult, and you know right from wrong. You want to be a technician, because someone has convinced you that it is a great and rewarding career. For the purpose of book, I will be talking mostly about the HVAC/plumbing industry, but these concepts apply to other industries as well. You may even have a business degree. I hope they taught you the legal and financial concepts related to running the business. I am sure they did not teach you any of this.

For the sake of this story, you are a great and skilled HVAC technician who is well loved by all of your customers. You can fix anything. There is no one faster or better than you, and you pride yourself on your knowledge of the mechanical code and the science that makes HVAC work. You know that air flow is critical to proper forced air heating and cooling, and you make fun of the guy who adds refrigerant when suction pressure is low, without an air flow check. You understand combustion and can find a carbon monoxide leak or problem in light speed. *You are hired.* Wait, you want to run your own business? That is a different animal that will require you to make the leap of faith and put yourself on a small branch that could collapse at any time.

But I can fix anything, and I am the best there ever was—much like Johnny, who beat the devil with his fiddle. Do you think that eventually the devil won? I guarantee that while Johnny was a better fiddle player, he did not have all the tools to defeat the devil on every front. Now you are in a different contest. It is not a bad thing to be technically strong and the best in your industry. I would much rather be the best technically and not a rip-off artist, but it's also important to be a great problem solver, be profitable, and be a leader in the community and the industry.

How much are you worth? Is the skill your only asset? You may have made it your goal to be better than the other technicians or businesspeople you respect. Did you learn about cash flow, accounts receivable, human resources, fleet management, marketing, inventory control, and all the other items with which you are not tasked?

When I went into business for myself in 1988, in our town a service call was $30 per hour. I realized at that time that I did not have the overhead of the other companies in town, as I was a start-up in a garage with a 1974 Chevy half-ton truck and a wrecked phone company service body for which I paid $250. I could charge $26 or $28 per hour and be the low-cost Walmart spread. Then I realized that I was as good as, if not much better than, all the others. Why did I not charge what they did? So I too settled on $30 per hour. That sounds like starvation wages, but I made good money and invested back into the company, and we are now doing around $1.9 million in an area of fifteen thousand in the whole county. We do, however, charge more now than we used to. That truck, by the way, was the first one in our area to be lettered, and it had a nice paint job, although it was fourteen years old.

We are individuals who protect the health of the nation, and we control the weather or wrangle lightning on a daily basis. Think about that. We do not just prescribe amoxicillin when our patients are not feeling well; we actually perform surgery and provide a healing touch to the ill and dying. We perform life-altering transplants, and we are the go-to guys for all things HVAC. We do not say we "practice" HVAC; we actually perform and cure ills guaranteed. What is that worth?

As a technician you have adopted a belief that you can fix anything, and folks want what you think they need. I used to think a toilet that cost $200 in 1988 was ridiculous. I still think a $1,200 toilet is a little crazy, but if you want one, I am your guy. I was given a Kohler K-500 design manual by a supplier. When asked to bid on a bathroom set out on a roughed-in basement bathroom, I priced the $75 toilet and a $35 lavatory with the chrome faucet that was only $50 at the time. I produced a proposal with all of those fixtures included, and the client wanted to see some pictures of what he could buy. "Okay, but I only priced the cheap stuff. Here it is." This $1,000 bath set was turned into a $2,500 job, and all I did was sell more expensive stuff. Why would a guy want the polished brass faucets and the $100 lavatory or the $200 toilet? But he did, and then he had me change his kitchen sink to a $400 unit and all the faucets in his upstairs bath to match the downstairs, and the toilet upstairs to match as well. Wow! I guess I really do not know what everyone wants, even if I am the best there ever was.

I still steer customers to what I consider the best option for them, but I no longer just sell good-quality but cheap stuff, because everyone buys heated leather seats in the cars they drive. And the luxury of AC in a car in 1965, when I was ten, is now standard in all vehicles that I have purchased in the last fifteen years. My 1966 Corvette was a factory air car with leather seats, which was very rare, and in my 2008 car it was standard, as were the leather seats.

If you have a boiler and you want to change your water heater from a conventional residential unit that is beside your boiler to a tank less, I will usually steer you to a side-arm tank, which will produce about the same hot water and be an easier install with similar results. But this will be a high-quality version that is stainless steel and has proven to be a great investment for anyone for whom we have installed them. I will not, however, say, "Let's just put a new one of what you have," like I have seen some people do.

Now you pull up to a house that is very modest. A widow lives there and needs a new faucet in the lavatory. You are a really good person and want to help the elderly woman, but you have just started your business and you are not a rich businessman. When I was just a one-man shop, I was called to a house to replace a faucet on a wall-hung lavatory for an elderly widow. This is normally a simple forty-five-minute job at the longest, but the old faucet was seized, and I had to remove the lavatory, clean it up, reinstall it, and caulk it all back in. I literally worked with sweat on my brow for about two hours. Feeling sorry for the owner, I charged her my cost for the faucet and $15 for labor, or 25 percent of what I would normally charge for labor. I handed her the invoice, and she commented that things were "sure expensive these days" and pulled her checkbook out of her purse. I am not a snoopy individual, but as I watched her write a check, I saw that she had over $7,000 in that account alone, which at the time was more than I had anywhere in any account. Boy, did I feel stupid. I could have taken my company to bankruptcy if I continued this practice.

Sometimes as a technician you may think that the boss is making big bucks. While the bill was $200, you made only $60 and did all the work. But remember that he also pays for a lot of unseen costs. If you think that you can do the $200 job for $60, then you will be another former small shop that calls me for a job as you starve to death.

I spoke about mentors before, and when I decided to go into business I went to Denver and visited a man for whom I had worked on a job at the Hayden power plant four years before. I told him of my plans, and he called his partner in from the other office and introduced me to him, explaining that I had worked for them in Hayden and I was going into business for myself. After his partner left, he told me how they had started and how much he wished that he was my age and helping me to start this business with him. It was an exciting time, and he yearned for those challenging days. He also told me that he had watched at least one hundred techs walk out his door, and before the door struck closed he could tell who would make it and who would not.

"Dave, you got the stuff. Here is my card. If you ever need anything, call. If you want to quit, call. I'll talk you down, because you can make it. I know it, and it is worth it." I never called for help, but I did visit him once, and we talked. I told him where I was, and he showed me where he was. Bud always comes to mind when things are tough. I hear him say, "You got the stuff." He is no longer with us, but he is still a part of my thought process. Do you have "the stuff"?

When I first opened my business, I was often told that the cost of workers' compensation and increased liability was just too much. Many business owners have run scams to try to escape paying for these benefits. While I would never tell you that the cost of those necessities is not ridiculously high, it is a cost of doing business, and you have to find a way to pay for it.

Many times we focus on the actual money we hand out and not what it costs us to be a skinflint. I have a friend whose brother was a trucking owner/operator, had his own truck, and lived four hours away in Denver. The exhaust system on his truck needed some welding, and he had been quoted $180 for this service in Denver. My friend's son-in-law was a welder at the power plant and could weld it for "free." The truck had to get to our town and back with a fuel mileage of around six miles per gallon and diesel at a cost of around $4.00. Every six miles cost $4.00. At a total of around four hundred miles round trip, the "free" welding job just cost $266.66 in fuel, not to mention tire wear and all the other costs that were not tracked.

This seemed absurd, and I would have never made that decision unless I wanted to come here for a reason. Then cost would not be a concern.

While we were on the city council, the water department manager presented a proposal from the water meter company to buy $50,000 worth of new meters that were remote read and did not require anyone to actually read them each month. If we made this purchase, they would give us the program for the new meters. I wanted to change all the meters in our town. At the time, we relied on each customer to read and write down the usage each month. Most customers estimated it and gave an actual number every three months or so. No city or county building was metered, so even if we did not want to exchange money for the water used, we had no idea how much was being used to water the parks or service any other building on our system. We knew we produced around 8 percent more water than we sold. Where did that go? All municipal systems have underground leaks, but 8 percent is really high, and we did not know if we leaked that or watered parks with it.

It seems like a no-brainer when you look at it from an armchair quarterback position. It is easy to make the call from there. It was different to decide to spend well over $1 million to install these meters. After we did, we paid off the bond two years early, the water department revenues increased dramatically, and we were getting paid for water we produced. A former mayor had to pay several thousand dollars in back water bill payments, since he had been estimating his motel for years, and now we were in better shape than we had ever been. We were one of the first cities in our state to have these meters. All water meters were read from two locations on hills with the suitcase computer we were given for buying the water meters. We did not have to hire two or three meter readers to make this happen. Twenty-two years later, our local gas and electric companies are just now using remote-read meters for the product they deliver.

The sad note is four of the council members (myself included) were faced with a recall election, and all were retained. As far as I am concerned, it is the best decision we made in the nine and a half years I spent on the council.

You will be forced to make decisions every day, and you can either make a "stinkin' thinkin'" decision or be a groundbreaking leader.

Do you have it? Can you fix it? I think you can, but you must be open to what can be done. We all have a tendency to say, "Well, that works in New York, but it will not work where I live." That is like a saw saying the wood is much softer in New York than it is in Colorado, and I could saw much better there. Or the bird says the air is much lighter in Oklahoma than it is in Idaho, and it could fly much farther there. The grass is always greener on the other side of the fence, particularly if you do not water and fertilize your grass. Your thinking will always be hampered by excuses if you let it. While some may be valid in your mind, none of them are actually the obstacles we make them out to be.

At sixty-three, I no longer like to go into crawl spaces or kneel in front of a furnace or boiler for an hour while I fix it. I still enjoy the challenge, but my legs cramp and go to sleep, and I can barely get back up. Why is that? I am not in technician shape anymore. If I wanted to overcome this, I could embark on an exercise regimen and maybe even have some procedure that would relieve this pain. I choose not to, because I do not have to, as I make my living by managing my business. As a young tech, you will think that working harder will be your financial savior, and you will not need to think about how to manage your business, because that in your mind is as painful to you as to kneeling is to me. It is not as I will probably live and be just fine without ever working on a furnace again with maybe the exception of the one that heats my house. You, however, will not survive just working harder and not paying attention to the changes in your thinking. You must change and evaluate what it means to be successful in business for yourself. I am a firm believer that you will fail if you do not. The wood where you live is the same as the wood where I live. Instead of making excuses as to why it will not work, look for ways that it *will* work.

Many people will ask for lots of money for this change in your thinking. While it is worth its weight in gold, no matter what you pay for the advice, it will be worthless if you do not act on it. For years I have wanted to lose weight. I finally decided that I will never lose weight by watching an infomercial about another weight-loss product. All of them might work, and if I employed half of them, I would weigh fifty-seven pounds. I am six feet one inch, but I am a long way from fifty-seven pounds. It will make no difference who you sign up with if you do not change your thinking. Some programs are better than others, but that is the difference in the mix. You can spend $25,000 per year or attend as many meetings as there are weeks and resorts to go to, but if it does not create change, you will actually be better off not spending the money.

I did not change with only one meeting or one summit or even one book. I changed with many, and each one cultivated the ground that is my thought process and helped me to be a better businessman and a better manager. It has been a process, and I share that with you to help you realize that it is a process worth your time and money. It will change your life and your heart, and it is worth it to take on as an endeavor.

Do you have the stuff? I do not know, but this is some of the stuff you need that did not readily exist when I started. Or if it did, I did not know where to get it. I believe that an honest, work ethic–driven, thoughtful individual has the beginnings of the right stuff. If that is you, let's go.

Keep the Faith, Baby

While I think about my time as a contractor, I have to reflect on what I have been through since I started my business and even before, when I was employed by someone else. While it is easy to say that times are changing, it is also imperative that we reflect on the history of our great nation.

I am not happy with the direction in which we are going. When I was ten the world I lived in did not look like it does today and my sense of right and wrong does not fit what we see now. However, I look at the way we have changed in this great country and feel the need to discuss our ability to mentally weather the storms to come.

Many successful business owners begin to adopt very radical views of life. One such story outlines a business that stopped taking all credit cards and began to preach the new doctrine to anyone who came into the dining room. Even stating at one time the outlandish notion that the jet trails you see were poison and that the federal government knew this and planned it. While we could argue that the pollution possibly caused by this is a poison, we have to recognize that belief is based on paranoia. The result was the closing of the business and the surrender of the deed to the bank in lieu of a payment. This is an example of a total failure of a good business that did not stay focused on what was important.

Why did I tell you this story? Over the years I have heard different folks tell me that "if this happens we are all sunk" about many things. One party told me that if Bill Clinton is elected, my business would fail. That did not happen. I have seen the effects of bad leadership at every level of government, and I can track the time we lost control of many of the truths we hold self-evident. Freedom today looks different than it did thirty years ago, but that should not move you to make the wrong decision in your business.

On September 10, 2001, I attended a Monday-night football game, the first at the new stadium in Denver, with our opponent, the New York Giants. Ed McCaffrey broke his leg, and I remember thinking the season was over in the first game, as he was a playmaker. I drove home after the game and slept in on Tuesday morning, the eleventh. When I got up and started getting ready to go to work, I turned on the TV and saw pictures of the World Trade Center and the planes flying into it. This was a terrorist attack on our home soil and not an official act of war. Many things changed overnight, and yet we were still working.

Now I mourn this event and think about how it changed our lives as Americans. What a tragedy. Eighteen years later, we are feeling the results of this tragedy. Historic events change many things in our lives. We choose to either take those lemons and make lemonade or allow them to bring us to a total defeat.

You are the captain of your ship. If you think that every captain has not seen stormy weather, then you have not been raised with a sense of any reality. Every business has suffered hard times. The difference is whether they strengthen you or defeat you.

Many believe the unrealistic myth that everything will be fine no matter what we do or what happens to us. That is not true, and how we choose to address hard times must be founded on truth. Most business failures are caused by an owner's mistaken ideas. Notice I did not say "mistakes"!

All businesspeople make mistakes—regarding whom or when they hire or fire, chasing the wrong customer, not releasing employees soon enough, among a myriad of other problems. Problematic thinking will devastate your business more than all of these mistakes.

I have witnessed many owners decide that the world was against them or that they had the world by the tail and they were invincible. Both ideas are on opposite ends of the truth. Here is a question for you to consider. Do you have the stuff? Part of the stuff we have discussed is the ability to hold your emotions in check and not let them affect your intelligence. When times are tough, you will be down, but will you commit business suicide? When times are good, you will be up, but will you spend yourself into oblivion?

I am not saying that the national or even local politics will not have an effect on you or your business, but that should not be the reason you lose your grip on reality. As I shared with the restaurant owner story, she did not have any reason to do what she did. It was just a total reaction to paranoia that created a series of events that took all the revenue and customers from her business.

Over the years I have acted as an "angel investor" to several small-business owners who were much younger than me. When times are good, they live below the times, and when times are bad, they have the resources to last them out. This is due to saving up in the good times, much like the pharaoh of Egypt did at Joseph's direction in the Old Testament—a biblical lesson that all business owners need to learn.

The ability to think and plan past a perceived problem will always be a skill you have to master. We watch each election cycle as many things change in all political arenas. If we swing with each of them, we will suffer sure and utter destruction. As I said earlier, the emotional response to 9/11 was that we were all doomed, and our freedom and way of life were over. Although I do not have anyone to ask who lived then, I am sure that all Americans felt the same way on December 7, 1941.

This nation is an experiment in democracy, and we have been given a republic by our forefathers. They even charged us to keep it if we could, and so far, for the most part, we have kept it. You have to ground yourself in truth.

All good HVAC techs and business owners realize that with modern equipment, a solid ground is imperative for operation. That green wire must connect the unit to solid Mother Earth ground through the electrical system, or this furnace or rooftop unit will surely not be able to ignite or operate correctly. You are just as dependent on your grounding. Do you always seek and rest in truth? When times are rough, do you believe that this too will change? Can you place your emotions in check and deal with the storm? These questions will define if you are grounded or not. We read in the New Testament that "you shall know the truth and the truth shall set you free." What does that mean to you? What is the truth? What is the truth about your present storm?

Any time we can place truth in our minds and hearts, we will gain from that a better understanding of what we should do and how we should act toward any storm or even any period of peace and advancement. Truth should be all around you. Another New Testament passage declares that, from the surroundings and the things we see in creation, we should know that there is a God. Does your musical taste promote your grounding in truth?

We are usually held to a standard that all our music has to be faith-based or religious in nature. I submit two popular songs that will change your life and your perception of truth. Let's explore them.

1. "Cats in the Cradle." Here is a song that appears in the seventies. Today it is one of my favorites. It is the story of a father and how he was so busy at work that he did not provide the time his son needed. Later, the son was just like him. How much better would our society be if all fathers and mothers took this to heart and spent time with the children with whom they were charged? I look at my relationship with my own son. While I was a single parent with a start-up business, I am sure that had an effect on his life and worldview. My involvement today with the youth of our community is based on my desire to see children and even young businesspeople have that input as they grow.

2. "I Want a New Drug." This song from the eighties by Huey Lewis describes the relationship that is shared with his significant other and how, when he is with her, he feels the emotions and support that was intended by God in the Garden of Eden when Eve was created for Adam. What a different world we would live in if this existed between spouses, and how much better off our youth would be if adults were not running around, looking for a thrill. One line states, "I want a new drug that makes me feel like I feel when I'm with you." It makes me understand the relationship and support that were intended in the Garden of Eden. If we all sought that, rather than how our world operates today, we would be better off as a society.

Many people have never listened to either of these songs with a mindset of seeking truth. I challenge you to take a good, hard look at your musical tastes and see if they add to or detract from your grounding plane.

The folks with whom you associate are also a great source of grounding and truth. You must cultivate those if you want to move forward. I am talking about not only finding mentors but also guarding your heart and mind from negative influences that will take away your grounding.

For many years I have dealt with several people who, from time to time, ask me to land them back on the ground. They do not ask me that when they call, but it is usually a call for help ("I am distraught and do not know how to proceed"). One good example is a friend of mine who was going through a divorce and usually takes all things in stride. He was unusually disturbed one day, as the divorce and property separation were not going as well as he had hoped. Divorce is a difficult thing at best. When coupled with an attorney's request to ignore what the former marriage could financially produce, it became devastating to him. The real situation was not as dire as it seemed. When not in the middle of the fight, it was easy to see the answer and make an informed decision based on the truth of the finances. Have you ever heard the saying, "It is hard to see the forest for the trees"? Most of the time we are not grounded enough in the truth of a situation, so it is easy to lose faith and direction.

There have been times I needed someone else to hold me to that as well. When they did, I moved forward, made the right decision, and kept my goal and path open to move ahead.

Relationships are a great grounding plane for your ability to keep the faith. I have several friends I cherish from my childhood. One of those is a friend with whom I have kept in touch, on and off, for most of my life. Another is someone with whom I recently reconnected. He is going through a hard time. On our first meeting, he told me he had been praying that God would send him some friends he could talk with and maybe even someone from his past. I told him God has a cruel sense of humor, since he sent me.

You may go through a divorce, the death of a spouse or loved one, a business downturn, daily stress, or many other things that make you want to quit. It may even be time for you to exit the business. I believe that there is a time for rest and relaxation and peace, even if that means being away from the business. Your escape can be by methods other than death. That being said, no one wants to exit due to total failure or the circumstances of their life being too much to handle.

I am a firm believer that the desires of your heart really do not change. When people say they do, it is an excuse to get out of a situation they never wanted to begin with. The reason we discussed the desires of your heart is to count the cost of business and make an informed decision to take on this challenge.

Once you've made a decision, you may be struggling with the daily pressures you are encountering. Is your struggle brought on by your lack of attention or from outside the business? Is a relationship making you want to give up?

I mentioned Bud and how he gave me his card and told me to call if I got discouraged. He would talk me off the ledge. I offer that to you now. Evaluate where you are in life. Do not give up until you have exhausted all options and found no other path. That means you need to have mentors to talk to. You will gain great strength from them.

Many times you may be ready to throw in the towel, or you think you are, and a well-placed discussion brings you to reality. Cultivate those relationships, and access them in these times. I deal with a young general contractor who is very good. He is ever attentive to his family, and they take many great trips together. His business has afforded him this luxury. While he has taken many more vacations than I have, I do not begrudge him this luxury. I actually admire how he relates to his family. Several years ago, two employees in whom he had placed a lot of trust decided they were going into business for themselves and leaving his company. They told friends how he was not a very good boss. I was told that by a mutual friend and when they shared that with me I reminded her that everyone that had ever left her authority as a boss or mine all said we were not good at being a boss. I had the opportunity to remind both her and this contractor that this was an attitude of many employees and usually it shows those employees short comings and lack of dedication to the business.

This young man was very disturbed by this and said to me, "I am going to go find a job somewhere and not deal with this." I was able to then address that he could not take the time off that he did from another job. I did not want him to work for me, as he was gone too much to be productive to me. I then informed him that these guys were probably not as great an asset as he had claimed. I encouraged him to put on his big boy pants and his tool belt and get in the field for a month or two to resurrect his business. He has thanked me for that pep talk many times. One of his good clients informed him that they were glad these two were gone. Things are not as we believe but rather as they are.

He is now back to normal. He hired another contractor who could make a crew work but could not manage a business. Together they are much better than either one was apart. The new guy gets more done than these other guys did and raises the level from his other employees. In return, my contractor friend is able to run the business well and support his revived staff. All is well.

Where would he have been if he had fallen prey to his emotions and tried to become an employee? I don't think that would have been a good thing for him.

Keeping the faith is about a dedication to truth and the building of a support system that holds you accountable to be the businessperson you decided to be when you dealt with the desires of your heart. If you are based in truth and have the desire to achieve excellence, you will be tested, and you will need a support system, which could include your family, friends, mentors, and even banker or accountant. Build on a solid foundation, or I am sure you will crumble.

Service Taught Like Your Grandfather Did It

My wife and I went to a restaurant last week that, in the past, had been a great place to eat with great service and very good food. We went at my suggestion to "go somewhere different." We recently purchased a house in a larger city that we plan to move to and live out our remaining years. It is in a warmer climate in a larger town but still has the small-town feeling.

I had a discussion with a service manager of a local car dealership, as we were having breakfast at a local restaurant. We ran out of coffee, and I have always believed that, in the breakfast restaurant world, taking the top off the coffeepot and setting it on the table was the international sign for "I need more coffee." In the good old days, when the pot had a tilt-up lid, that was the sign. I marvel at the times servers in this establishment walked past and did not notice that we were out of coffee. My friend mentioned that great service is what our dads taught us growing up. Since most of these servers were at least two generations removed from me, I figured it was their grandfather who would have taught them this and that their father had failed to pass this on, or maybe he was not present during their lives.

I had called ahead to make a reservation, and we arrived at or before the appointed time. We were seated and asked if we wanted drinks, which we ordered. Then we both proceeded to order the filet and gave our salad dressing request. Our salad was presented with a small basket of bread thankfully. We finished the salad and bread and waited for our steaks. Almost one hour later we were confronted with

"I am sorry, but when I sent your order to the kitchen, it did not send." This server had passed our table many times, and it never occurred to anyone that maybe there was something wrong, as the same server had served others who were seated after us. No one took the time to provide an excellent experience for us, as customers. By the way, we are not the complaining type. They were focused on the menial task at hand to move plates from the kitchen to the tables of those that evidently the computer told them were ready to be served was the only focus in this dining room. Apparently it was not evident to them that we had not received any food in over an hour. What a disappointment we had, and we will probably not return unless someone else invites us to go there and is paying the bill.

Interestingly we had a new steam shower door installed that morning by a great company in this city. Don was very pleasant and installed a beautiful product with skill and precision we would expect only from a brain surgeon. I called his office to tell them how pleased I was with the product and service, and the receptionist was surprised and asked, "Is that the only reason you called?" This shows you I am not normally the customer who complains and looks for a handout. We also had electrical work, carpet, and tile installed in this home, and those were great experiences as well.

Since I have over thirty years of offering HVAC and plumbing services, I've thought about the industry that has allowed me to buy a house in another city and build the garage I've always wanted on that property. The things I did as I started to offer this business that for some reason were built into my character or DNA by my parents are not in our society any more. To create a great service experience in our world today we must take the time to teach what their daddy did not. A phrase that a good friend of mine always uses but normally in the context that we cannot teach them what their daddy did not. I think to survive we must teach that to all of our team.

Many years ago, when we all charged a one-hour minimum because that is what everybody charged, I was called to repair a leak on a washing machine connection. Upon arrival I inspected the connection and found the packing nut on both the hot and cold shut-off valves needed a little tightening. A six-inch crescent and four minutes later, the job was complete. Wham! One-hour pay, and on to the next item. Instead of just saying, "There you go. That will be forty dollars," I asked if there was anything else they would like me to look at, as I had an additional fifty-five minutes or so that I could spend with them. They looked at me with amazement and said no, that was the only real problem. Those people became long-term customers. I was willing to look for the sign of "I need more coffee" or look for the table whose order wasn't ready.

In our society, we believe we must protect ourselves, and we always believe someone is out to get us, so we complain before we have a problem. Also, we are not focused on any career paths. Each day we work is just another paycheck. Our performance is not based on dedication or the idea of serving our fellow man. We have become a selfish nation and only want to serve our fellow man when we get something in return. The idea of "It is better to give than to receive" is lost on our society today. Every industry shows it in their customer service.

We constantly hold up the banner of "It is our right." While this nation was built on freedom, it was also built on respect of our fellow man and the idea that we lose our rights when we violate others'. Here is a question for you. When we did not receive our steak in less than one hour, did our server have a "right" to a tip? Was my right to have an enjoyable dinner out with my wife violated by the server's slothful service and attitude? I was still going to pay for the meal, and I did leave a less-than-normal-for-me tip. Reflecting back on that experience I am not sure why I left a tip at all. My mother who waited tables for most of her early adult life always said a tip is for great service as they are paid to be here.

What about the owner of the restaurant who placed this person in the position to take care of his customers and be well paid for excellent service? While I feel sorry for him, when I was offered an additional free glass of wine or dessert as compensation for the mistake, I left with the belief that I would never return again. Is that fair to the owner? Did this server cost him a new and probably loyal customer?

Have I, as a service tech, provided this type of service? Should I be upset when every customer does not return due to our service? Ask yourself these questions: "Have I always attempted to provide good service?" "Do I create loyalty?"

If you are an owner or service manager, ask yourself these questions: "Do I keep track of the performance of my staff?" "Do I equip and empower them to perform?" "Do I have their best interests in mind?"

No matter which side of the equation you are on, you may see that you are at fault. If you are a tech and cannot answer the questions with a yes, then it may be time for some personal examination and changes. These can even be if you are working for a company that does not provide you the backing you need. If you want to be a servant-minded tech, maybe you need to change companies.

While I really do not blame the owner of the restaurant for the lack of service, it is possible that they are responsible for the poor performance of this server. (By the way, the steak was very good, but by the time I was able to eat it, anything would have been great.) As the principal of any business, you must make a profit from the sweat of your staff and not their blood. If you are paying a fair wage and really want to make them better with benefits and good working conditions, you have to also look at the teamwork among your staff. Do you have team members who suck the life out of their fellow workers? Are there staff members who are making about the same wage and not performing? Maybe you felt sorry for them and gave them a job, and now you cannot bring yourself to make the change.

I once came close to closing my business due to an error that the office manager made. She had again failed to register our corporation with the state. My wife had resolved this problem several times before, but she had not caught this one. There were many other issues as well, but this one made me take action. When I found out that Colorado did not recognize our business as a corporation due to our failure to send in the required form and small fee, I was depressed. Not knowing what the implications were, I was prepared to close the business and go find a job. After a period of time alone, I realized that not only was this one employee about to have a negative effect on me and my family, but she was going to put seven or eight other families out of work as well and take a service from our community that I had always felt needed to be here.

That was when I decided to terminate that one person. As a result, the entire company was healthier. A cancer was gone, and we could now begin to heal. It was a very difficult thing for me, as I normally treated my staff as members of the family and felt responsible for their continued employment and ability to feed their families. I still attempted to provide for the employees, but now I view them as a living organism instead of individuals. While I do not believe I ever became the boss who just fired people at random, I learned that there were some hiring mistakes that needed to be rectified. For some reason, some folks who were great in the beginning were now a negative and life-sucking drain on the business, myself, and all the other staff.

I relate this story to emphasize the need for all owners and managers to not only serve their fellow man and create an environment that encourages the type of service our grandfathers taught but think of your staff as a living organism and realize that the whole needs to be more than the sum of its parts. If you have staff members who are not performing at a level require, or they create drama or tension, maybe it is time to place them in your employment relocation department and decide to remove the cancer. I think you will find that the dollars that you spent on them to infect your company would have been better used as fire starters.

Not only are they detrimental to the production of the other staff members, which consumes company resources, but you are probably paying for efforts from which you are not receiving any production. Across the board this is a dangerous situation. Government operates like that, and I hope your goal is to not be like government.

Think about this as you perform your daily tasks. Make this a focus of your company or your focus as an individual. I guarantee you will like the way it works. To date, I have never witnessed the removal of a bad employee that did not make the others happier or change their dedication to the company. When we allow an individual to test and break out of our fences, we invite the entire company to go off the rails. Chaos is the typical result.

Early in my career, I was hired on to a power plant as a pipe fitter/welder. Upon passing my test, I was taken to the work area by my new foreman, a man for whom I have the greatest respect. To this day I consider him a friend. While walking to the work area, he turned to me and told me whom he was putting me with and then said in his English accent, "See if you can pick him up a bit." I was going to work with an individual who I had known for quite a while and who I knew was not productive. As you can imagine, I was not happy about this but decided to see what I could do. After two weeks of pushing this individual, my foreman came by one day while he was gone, and I asked how we were doing. His response was "Unbelievable." How much better could we have done if I could have concentrated on the actual task and not on managing my work partner to get the job done?

I have never believed that a crew of all-stars works well together, as the 76ers proved that. They had a roster of the best the NBA offered but could not win a championship, as they were not a team. As long as you, as an employer, continue to make excuses for nonproductive or difficult employees, you will never have a team. You may have winning streaks that make you believe you are headed for the championship, but your season will be far from over. In 1972, the Miami Dolphins were the only undefeated team to ever win the Super Bowl. Few people were considered greats at the time, and even the backup quarterback played a major portion of the season that year. The bottom line is that if they are difficult and not productive today, they will probably not change. Ultimately they may cost you a good and productive employee who might take you to the Super Bowl.

Most contractors at one time or another were in the field as techs or installers before deciding they could make it big on their own. Look back at how you would have felt if your boss had asked you to work with the guy who nobody else wanted to work with. Would you have been happy? That might be one of the reasons you left to start your own firm. Why would you impose that on an employee who is productive for you today? If you did not like that, why would they? By the way, I worked for that company for only a short while. As soon as I could, I left for a different contractor on the same project and moved into supervision. I hoped to never work with a guy like that again.

It is your company's and, more importantly, your responsibility to keep your crew productive. The delay in dealing with an employee who is not productive is detrimental to your company's health and productivity.

Commit today to making your company great, and always remember that "good is the enemy of great." We tend to think that good is enough, as no one wants to be considered "bad." If we look in the mirror of our company and decide we are good enough, we have reached our peak of performance. As long as that satisfies you, that is all you will be.

Being in a small market, I realized early on that we would not have a lot of competition. Have you ever noticed that great competition breeds great competitors? I had to go outside of my local area to find other contractors, and I had to work up to their level. This proved to be the best thing I could do for the company and our productivity.

Remember that we are talking about service like our grandfathers did it. I can only believe that the guys from years ago held themselves to a high level of service and competency, as that was what the United States was built on at that time. We have become complacent as a nation, and that leads to just being good enough and not performing at our highest capacity.

It is perfectly acceptable to be critical of your company's or team's performance and point out those issues. When you point them out, three fingers are pointing back at you. Ask these questions: "Am I the reason we are not more productive?" "Do I portray a productive ability and dedication to my part of this company?" Your organization will only grow to be as strong as you are willing to grow your ability to manage and create the culture that is one of productivity. The great employees will cherish a position in a company like that. The mediocre members of your team who are allowed to stay around will only poison the rest of the team. One bad apple *does* spoil the whole bunch.

You have to show dedication to the company that you desire from your employees, or you are doomed to have a team as unproductive as you are. When you constantly "forget" or "have not gotten to it yet," why should any other team member not emulate that action?

Many managers think that the job is to change the company to offer new products, procedures, or ways to do things. Without the dedication to the established operation these are only a feel good effort to make the manager happy about their performance. Did I really say that? Yes, I did. I have watched companies try to expand into new products or areas or change the way things were done to just make the manager feel good, and I have never witnessed a good result come from that.

Small-course changes are also problematic, though not usually life-threatening. The company that decides to expand service into drain line cleaning can have great rewards and also huge consequences. The company that has been HVAC-oriented in either construction or service or both that wants to take on plumbing can have the same result. While there can be rewards in anything, it will only come with extreme dedication, not with just starting the new venture and announcing it to the world.

That is how our grandfathers defined service. They became good at something and then worked to greatness, and then they became experts on all things in their chosen field. Today we seldom see the country doctor who treats everything, as specialists are the norm. I believe that is due to the modern lack of dedication and the desire to get a participation trophy in everything we do.

If you want to provide service like our grandfathers did, then you have to hold to their principles. There is no trophy for doing the minimum, only for excellence. Paul, in 2 Thessalonians 3:10, stated to this church that if they had folks in their group who would not work, they should not eat. This is the real basis of great service. If you are lazy and slothful, you will never provide great service. If you are a servant-minded individual and always ready to work, you will provide great service and be productive. You will reap the rewards of that in how you are compensated for your efforts.

Have you ever known someone who always has a problem? Maybe they lost their job, their home foreclosed, or they lost their car. Have you ever looked at how they approach life? As I end this chapter I recommend you take an honest hard look at your own personal attitudes and the actions that those attitudes create. That is to say they are suffering because of their own actions or slothfulness. Make sure you as an owner or manager do not fall into this trap.

Think about how to provide great service at every level in yourself and your company. It is the only way I know to succeed and live a fruitful life.

Capitalization

Capitalization is an ugly word that most do not understand. Hopefully I can shed some light on the attitudes that create financial ruin for many contractors across this country. I am always intrigued by the number of new contractors who land their first "big" job and think that they now have that much money to spend. You will probably not profit more than 10 percent on your first job (and maybe not that much).

The same mind-set holds true when you look at your profit and loss statement and see that you are on track to gross 10 percent more than last year. That is not a reason to spend that much money, as you may spend that much in the growth. We were in a growth mode for several years before cash flow really took off. While we bought a lot of new trucks and equipment, we were able to catch up and put money in the bank after about three years. By the way, I did not use a revolving line of credit, and there is nothing wrong with that, as long as you are not overextended.

My first pipe machine was a Ridgid 300 with no options. It was probably a 1965 model that I bought in 1988 and used for twenty-seven years. I installed a lot of jobs with it. I think I paid $500 from an old retiring plumber in Kansas City, and that included several other items. The same machine with the options is now around $4,000 and will not thread pipe (unless you know what you are doing) any better than my $500 antique.

How much better off as a one-man shop was I to use this machine as long as I could? At the time I did not understand how to do this to take the tax advantages. I did not purchase a new machine with the "I need to own this" mind-set. Believe me, there are items that you need to own but not when you are a one-man shop. You should always be aware of your company's needs. That can be a real boon to your profit margin. For instance, we own two pieces of equipment that I never thought we would buy. One is a Nytek layout table for which we spent $8,000 in 1999 and have used for seventeen years. This table has made sheet metal fabricators out of guys that had never done this and guys who are really fast in the shop now. Another purchase was our scissor lift that I purchased used from a rental company, and it has been a real boon to us. The job that would take a total of three days with scaffold now takes one day with the lift, and I profit the savings. Make sure capital investment makes a greater profit for you and helps to grow the company.

I am not saying that a pipe machine is not a needed tool; it is just the thought of a new one of that cost that I question. Keep in mind that without the capital to survive hard times (and they will come), you will not be able to sustain a business. Many operate on bank money, which is an accepted practice. I am good with that for a short time, but the idea of needing a constant revolving line of credit is something I do not desire. You may need it to get started or to fund a big job or even for a downturn, but if you go to the bank for a constant bailout line of credit, you'll be doomed to fail. Eventually you will have to either pay the piper or convert this line to an actual loan and make payments for a long time.

It is in every technician's DNA the desire to own all the latest and greatest tools. That is also in most people's DNA. If it was not there, how could we explain the large tool section at Home Depot and Lowe's or the tools that are prominently displayed at any supply house? They are impulse purchases, and we all fall for them. With a new business, be careful to not fall prey to these desires. The one-man shop I talked about earlier had placed growth, advertising, training, and possibly profit behind the desire to own a new Ridgid pipe machine.

I have watched contractors from every trade purchase items they really do not need, which end up sitting with little use and never providing a profit to the company. I watched a carpenter purchase a complete cabinet shop. While he did some great wood projects, for the most part all of that equipment is taking up sawdust-infested space in his building and rarely is used.

While our Nytek is the best investment I ever made, there are times it just sits there. It is not a machine we use daily or even weekly, but when we do, it pays dividends. The scissor lift is a piece of equipment that we use often. Many times it will be parked on a job and stored there when we are not using it, but again it was used and has paid dividends to the company.

When you are starting out, there are certain items that you must have to perform your trade, and those are absolute necessities.

1. A reliable truck, and if you live where I do, one that is four-wheel drive
2. A service body, van, or other system to protect and organize your tools and materials
3. Hand tools to practice your trade
4. Accessories to allow you to manage your business, such as a computer and other office supplies
5. A cell phone and/or land line to take and respond to calls
6. Large tools, such as recovery machines, and other items that allow you to perform the work
7. A place to store materials (you will likely have leftover materials from jobs—it will amaze you how fast you gain leftover inventory and need a place to store it)

While the Ridgid pipe machine I mentioned earlier would fit into line 6 above, if you are not threading pipe every week, you do not need that machine. If you live in a large city, particularly in the South, you will probably not need a four-wheel-drive truck. You may prefer to have a van over a service body, and either can be purchased used to start out. Even some good toolboxes on a pickup can be made to work on the first truck.

Many times a new business secures a revolving line of credit from a local bank or some other financing institution. Be sure to use it for the intended purpose and not fund new toys or tools you *want* from this. Think of those items like I do my classic cars: never buy what you cannot pay for when it comes to toys. If you think you need a trailer, then buy a used one when you can pay for it and not when you want it with a line of credit.

When your business begins to grow, you will see cash to use for some of these items. Always be careful that these are items that will make the company more productive and are not just for the purpose of a tax deduction. It is easy to get into the "Write it off" mode and think that is making you money. Remember that you have to have a profit on which to pay taxes to make writing it off a good thing. While I have used my business purchases to keep my actual tax liability as low as possible, it is not a good practice to be left out of control. It can be like a credit card with a low monthly payment and a high balance. It is easy to think this is a great way to finance life.

With the time I have spent on a bank board, I have become familiar with the line of credit. After I attended a board meeting, I was making the forty-mile drive home and told the president of the branch in my town I thought I needed to create a line of credit. This was a banker who was more concerned with my success than his loan portfolio. He asked if I had a big job or needed equipment. When I told him that I just sort of felt like I must have been doing this wrong, he declined my request for a line of credit. I had basically bought all my sheet metal equipment and all my tools out of company profits for years and only financed new trucks when needed through the financing arm of my local Chevrolet dealer.

You can never borrow your way out of debt, but I am not averse to manageable debt. I like what Dave Ramsey says to our instant gratification society. I believe he is correct in this approach to the individual who does not worry about paying anything off. That being said, I am also not averse to incurring debt for a major purchase, particularly when the interest is low. I once financed a service body at 0 percent with GMAC when I bought a new truck for which I could have paid cash. Why would I use my capital when I could use theirs at no cost?

A friend of mine went through a divorce and had two car payments. He was worried sick about the payments, and I encouraged him to trade both vehicles for a new 2012 Chevrolet truck and finance his debt at 0 percent. It lowered his monthly payments, he drove a new truck, and he quickly was able to get back on track. It was a good use of credit. Having two car payments probably was not a good use of credit.

Many say that money is the root of all evil, but the truth is that the *love* of money is the root of all evil. We all see this every day. It is not just money that is the problem but also our desire to have things. It is freeing to learn that you can live without things. When you do that, having them means less to you than life itself. Paul said he had learned to abase and abound, meaning he lived in luxury and poverty and was able to live a happy life either way. You will only be able to finance your business when money is not the only factor. You must make a profit, or you will not be here tomorrow. When you build your business on a servant's heart with a will to do good in all you do, you have a greater capital position than many Fortune 500 companies.

You must have capital to begin, but to be well capitalized is as much about your attitude toward money as it is about the availability of it. Companies that fail from lack of capital probably really fail from their attitude toward money.

Early in the history of my business, I performed the plumbing, HVAC, and medical gas installation for a new dental clinic in town. It was quite an endeavor, and I had all the sheet metal provided by a subcontractor, while I provided all equipment and plumbing, as well as the installation of all the work other than the ductwork from the units. This was a $35,000 contract. We worked along with progressive payment requests and our final draw was around $10,000. This came at the end of the year. While we had performed our job and had very few extras, the general contractor had many. Rather than declaring those in change orders as we went along, the final bill was over the agreed amount. In the last bill the general contractor presented to the owner we were asking for our final payment request. It took several months to sort this out. About five months later I received my final payment. Now all my suppliers and subs were paid, and I was out any profit on this project, but somehow I managed to keep all things afloat and did not miss any payments or go out of business.

A few years later I had a similar situation. The business took a $57,000 hit, and again we were able to maintain and not suffer extinction. We were paid in about five or six months. Again I paid everyone I owed. You might think I was making so much profit that I could afford to do that. By the way, neither time did I borrow from the bank to stay afloat.

In 2009, when Barack Obama was elected as president, the busy time we had been experiencing came to a halt. In one year our gross revenues dropped $750,000. The previous year we were over $2.3 million, and that year we grossed $1.45 million. Again I did not miss any payments. I laid off only one individual who I really wanted to fire, and we again weathered the storm.

I attribute all three of these situations to the attitude that my wife and I had about money. It was more about the business than the profit, and that allowed for great profit in good times. I am sure there are many stories that have the same outcome, but there are exponentially more that end in defeat.

Is it a difference of market, dedication, luck, or attitude about money? I will leave that to you to decide for yourself. My market was small, and I have never considered myself to be lucky, though I believe luck does favor the prepared mind.

Make sure you manage your capital, and remember that a good name is far more desirable than gold. You cannot have a good name without managing capital. I have witnessed individuals who owe everybody, and the result is lost relationships and self-esteem. The end result is usually a paranoid defensive stance by the individual, who believes everyone hates them. The truth is everyone resents how they were treated, and they pity the individual for what they have done with their life.

If you need more capital to operate, remember that even a silent partner screams at you in your sleep. Find a way to be in control of your business, and manage your wealth that a business like this can provide.

Building a Crew

Many of the mechanical contracting firms were started by great technicians. The founders of those businesses survive and thrive based on how they transfer to the job of owner, CEO, and human resources manager. Many good individuals have been highly skilled at performing the tasks of their trade, be it HVAC, sheet metal, plumbing, or refrigeration. Those same folks can fail miserably if they do not progress into the manager of the business. In this chapter, we are going to deal with the concepts of building a crew. J. Paul Getty realized as a young man that the only obstacle to the amount of money he could make was the time he had to make it. Then he decided to create a company with a crew of producers.

When you set out to start a business or even buy an existing one, odds are you have been a foreman or a great lead technician, but you may have never been asked to bid on a job. You also may have had only one or two other techs who were your responsibility. Now you are faced with more work than you can handle and the need to clone yourself. To date, cloning has not been tried with any success, so that is not an option. The best you can hope for is to find some employees who will dedicate their time to you and have some team spirit that leads to a winning future.

Let's explore what you want to do with your business. Do you want to be a full-service company and offer both new construction and repair work in your business model? Maybe you do not want to provide service and think the guys who do are tied to their customers at the hip. Maybe you want the freedom to just do new construction and never handle anything that is not brand-new. Do you want to perform only HVAC or plumbing or refrigeration, or do you want to handle it all and even add electrical to the mix? All these are valid questions and need to be dealt with as you progress.

I had a young man's attitude. I thought I could do anything. I opened a one-man shop that performed new and service plumbing, HVAC service and replacement, along with new installation of hydronic heat, service on refrigeration, and new installation. My weakest point was sheet metal fabrication, but many furnaces had been installed and operated with factory duct and breakdown plenums. As my business grew, I added a plumber. Then I contracted with a sheet metal worker and later replaced him with my own equipment and employees. I hired a refrigeration tech and then expanded that to two or three full-time refrigeration and HVAC service techs. The company built profitably and with good quality control. We performed construction jobs as large as $300,000 and as small as a bathroom remodel with some heating changes. If it was plumbing, heating, cooling, or refrigeration, we did it and became the go-to guys in our small region. Your area may dictate how you can be the most profitable, in addition to your skills and desires. We will explore all the different areas as we move forward, starting with a construction-based company.

The construction-based company is doomed to play poker, where only the low hand wins, until a reputation of excellence takes that bidding exercise and makes it a budgeting one. To begin, you will be bidding on all kinds of projects and go from nothing today to needing a crew of ten tomorrow. While this did not appeal to me, I firmly believe that a small crew of employees who have the company's best interests at heart will profit from signing a contract with the trade union that matches the work you are doing. Many contractors today find crews to man jobs with this use. There are also online companies that will provide crews of people. Your central management team will be the key to your success. Those folks need to play for the team and not always be the superstars. Take a lesson from the 76ers, who had all the best players in the NBA and could never win a championship, because no one played for the team. The same is true for all portions of your business. You may find a superstar in the trade for which they are applying, but their lack of character will destroy any productivity. We should take a look at the Boy Scout creed and the character traits that are listed there. In case you are not familiar with this here are the twelve listed and we added four to our list of traits, in order: A Scout is Trustworthy, Loyal, Helpful, Friendly, Courteous, Kind, Obedient, Cheerful, Thrifty, Brave, Clean, Respectful, Consistent, Adaptable, Teamwork, and finally Competent. Let's take a situation and see how this plays into your operation.

A server had worked in the kitchen of a local restaurant as a cook and decided to work the serving side of the business. He happens to be one of the best servers this local restaurant has ever sent to my table. Under former management, he had requested five minutes off the floor to take care of a personal situation and was denied, so he chose to leave his shift five minutes early and was terminated for that action. That manager was replaced, and the new manager was tasked with rebuilding a crew. He hired this server back, and again he was one of the best they had ever had. The new manager was trying to right all the wrongs of the staff and change the culture of this establishment, which is not an easy task. One Saturday during a lunch rush, the kitchen manager (who was one of the problems) decided to hit another cook with a hot pan and then threw a fit and left. This left the manager without a full staff in the kitchen when the dining room was full. The server and former cook went to the back, put on cooks' aprons, and cooked them out of the jam. He did not receive the tips he would have on the floor, so he chose to take a cut in pay for that day and make sure the team could succeed. In doing this, he displayed at least three of the traits of the creed: loyal, adaptable, and the ability to work for the team. He could have just let them flounder and not participated. Wouldn't you want this type of individual on your team?

Maybe you want to have a fluid crew and complete projects, or maybe you want a static crew and just keep putting new construction ahead of them. If the economy allows for enough new construction to keep you busy and profitable without major travel, or if your business model is to travel to stay busy, you will still need to put a crew together that will have your best interests in mind. These employees do not need to be great at customer service, but they need to be honest and skilled in their trade, with a drive to perform to the best of their ability and "do it right." That saying creates a lot of conflict, as we tend to believe the way we do it is the only right way. In all reality, the result of proper system performance can be achieved with many optional installations. As long as the system works, the color of the flex or the type of fittings and pipe is left up to code compliance and not to our personal preference. The new construction contractor will need to be aware that time is money, and the use of proper materials and installation habits are keys to the success of that firm. Many times the construction job requires a relatively short-term crew and may last for only a few months. Personality conflicts will not have the effect that fifteen years of working for the same company will. Two employees who do not get along may never have to work on the same job again. While it is better if all play well with others, you can usually survive until the job is complete with this type of conflict. That being said, it is always better to be a team and strive to emulate that type of atmosphere no matter what you are doing or what type of business you are in.

Always remember that new construction was the first flat-rate pricing exercise and that, unlike service books for flat rate you create a new one for every job and depending on how much you want the job or do not want the job will also trigger your pricing matrix. If you need work for cash flow, you will be tempted to take 5 percent less in profit just to have the work. I was asked by a general contractor, when we suffered a work turndown in our area, if I was still bidding on jobs to make a profit. I was and did not get some of the jobs I priced.

The construction-only firm will always be in this mode and will only have the phone ringing to bid on other jobs. If you are lucky or maybe really good, you will land some projects just because it is your firm, but that does not happen for many years and only comes with a great reputation.

You can choose to only bid on residential, commercial, or even industrial work and limit your company in that way as well. All of these options are contingent on your economy, area, and desires. There is not a right or wrong answer here—just the need to focus and build toward that goal.

A construction-only contractor will always be limited by either travel, the local economy, or the building going on in that economy. Profits will rise and fall, similar to a those of retailers at Christmastime. A service-based business can be impacted by weather changes, both good and bad, and by the local economy, but the impact will not be as drastic as a construction-only contractor. I decided to diversify my business to create multiple levels of work and attempt to keep a full-service department that can fuel my installers and also bid on and contract new construction and also retrofit on a large scale.

This creates a need to have employees that are professional and able to communicate, as they may be on a service call today and installing in a new house tomorrow. While the ideas I expressed in the previous paragraphs are true for a construction-only business, all employees should be held to a standard that creates a professional atmosphere and provides your customer—a general contractor or a housewife—the same level of performance.

I have found that many times you can fill a position with any old sheet metal worker or plumber in the storm, but if they lack the professional attitude, you are only kidding yourself that they will maintain the level that satisfies them and you while serving your customer. I have hired individuals who came recommended and had credentials that made me think they were an actual godsend to my business, only to find out why they were looking for a job. I have also been successful in hiring young employees of good moral character and work ethic and training them in the skills they need to perform the tasks at hand. Training is key. You must engrain in them the way you want things done and how they should act with a customer. If they cannot get along with the other members of the crew, they will not get along with your customers.

The book *Good to Great* outlines the idea that the best-performing corporations in the United States all held a dedication to hiring talent if they found it and then preparing the task they would handle. An example is a good installer working in another industry who is tired of that job. It is not a bad idea to hire that individual and then bid on more work to provide the position for them. You may find that you have built a thankful and dedicated employee who has the skills you wanted. You could also approach this as they do in the NFL. We all see players cut that were at one time great, and now they cannot perform, or they have developed an attitude that limits their effectiveness. I am not one to just hire and fire, as many of our staff have been here multiple years, but I have been known to part ways with a problematic employee.

I have actually found an employee who was working for another plumbing or heating company and offered them a job but only because I was sure the other company was not taking care of them. If a potential employee has left several firms, you do not want to be another notch in their belt as they try out your firm. I have found they are best left outside of what we are trying to build.

Training is a key component to keeping your crew fresh, committed, and engaged. There is an old saying that if you train them, they will leave and become your competitor. I suggest that if you do not train, them they might stay, and that could be worse. Many individuals have worked for my firm in a town of ten thousand and started their own company. I terminated some of them for cause. They have not impacted us as much as they would have had I left them there to fester and infect the entire crew. Individuals with good moral character will rarely leave and try to get even with you unless you give them a reason. That could be low pay, poor conditions, conflicts with other employees, or personal conflicts with you. You may want to terminate them if you find they are no longer productive, and that is your decision. Making them leave because of the way they were treated should never be a situation you get into. Deciding to terminate because of their actions is good for the crew overall, but you need to be a leader to keep them engaged. I've always held to the concept that I should make money from the sweat of the employees and their efforts but not their blood.

Take the Boy Scout creed, not only for the actions of your crew but for your actions and those of your management team as well. I think you will find it works, and you can profit and perform a great service to any sector you decide to serve. As you build this crew, be aware of your strengths and weaknesses, and use this in your daily operation. Clint

Eastwood said, "A man's got to know his limitations." I think this is an important attitude to adopt and practice to keep you in check. If that does not work for you, try the commandment "love thy neighbour as thyself." You will never be a hated employer when you practice that, and you can look at yourself in the mirror. I am not saying there will never be an individual who will try to convince others that you were unfair to them, and they will usually be the one whom you should not have hired, or at least terminated years before you did, but the actual way you treat your employees will be known. Make the ones you want to keep desire to stay. Studies have shown that the actual money is the third or fourth item on the list of things that employees look for. High on that list is being challenged and respected and feeling valued.

Service-based contractors rely on their employees to interact with customers and provide a level of service that is second to none. This requires some training. It is not impossible to take a really good construction or installation tech and make them a service tech. Think of it like going to a doctor. The actual surgery or medical side of the experience can be spot-on, but bedside manner will make up your mind. I had back surgery about ten years ago, and the doctor came in with a black Armani suit, a white linen shirt, and a red power tie. He had on patent leather Florsheim shoes and no socks, with the whitest ankles I had ever seen (I am Italian and wear shorts most of the summer). At first, I was taken aback, but after he began to speak I knew this guy could fix me. I often have recommended this guy, who is two hundred miles from where I live, above the local back surgeon, as he did wonders for me. Your clients need to do the same for each tech you have. That is a growth situation that should never stop as you train in both technical and personal service.

All customers are just like you and like different types of people. When I am presented with a new group of people, I naturally gravitate toward those who like cars and football and really have no common ground with the big game hunters in the group. Your customers are the same, and the way to deal with that is scheduling and training for your staff. I can talk to hunters about anything, and while it is not my cup of tea, we can find the common ground we need to get the job done.

That is staff training, as you rarely have the opportunity to train your customers.

As you progress in building your business, take care to not forget the Boy Scout creed. As soon as you do, you will see why. The employee hired because of their technical strengths will soon make their presence felt with their character flaws.

I have addressed the two types of business models, and these are a pure attempt at either service or construction. In most markets you will have to operate on both sides of this equation. You may be strong in construction and perform very little service, but you always have to service the systems you install for the warranty period. Why not build a service business that takes care of those systems until they need to be replaced? Maybe you only want to do service, but many of your trusted clients desire some construction systems installed in a new house or commercial building. This is a good, natural way to start a construction crew. No matter what your local area is like, you can operate in both modes if you desire. I have found that today we are servicing many systems we installed fifteen years ago. We also complete remodels and new construction for clients for whom we began our relationship as their service contractor.

These ideas work for HVAC, refrigeration, and plumbing. And they work for a forced air contractor learning and installing hydronic heating, or a plumbing and hydronic firm installing forced air. Look at any field with the proper training and techs, and move forward in that. Just remember that the character of an employee should never be ignored, and the technical skills are not more important than the character of that individual. A character flaw will become evident and create more problems than a technical flaw, which can be trained away.

We just volunteered a Saturday at a local Fuller Center for Housing, which is the same idea as Habitat for Humanity. Our crew installed plumbing, heating, and gas piping, and together they spent a total of ninety hours there on one Saturday. Our local Village Inn bought us breakfast, and a caterer brought us ribs for lunch. It was a great crew-building experience for all who were there. All of them worked tirelessly for no pay. Giving of their time was a joy for them. I like to think that they all did that because they believe that they have received from the company and all that it does in this community. It was a pure symphony of plumbing and heating, and for the most part the rough-in is done. They all know that we are selling the materials to the Fuller house at our cost, which is a better cost than they could get anywhere. Because of our relationships, we have secured a free York furnace and Rinnai water heater and some Delta faucets for the house. All of those items were donated by our suppliers, with the help of the manufacturing companies. This is the second time we have performed this service, and it was great to watch.

I know that our staff is proud of their efforts and that they feel like a larger part of the community, because they were involved in helping someone less fortunate than they are. The family that has been chosen for this house is a single-parent mom with twin autistic children. Knowing that will reward our efforts more than anything.

In all of the discussion about building a crew, the underlying theme is to build one to meet your business plan. That probably will change over the years you are in business. As you build a business that reaches the mechanical needs of your area, you may find that you do things you never thought you would, to get a greater workload, to get more opportunity, or to fill a glaring void in the market. A good case for that would be deciding to offer drain line cleaning for a plumbing contractor, or possibly offering forced air systems to an area that is in grave need of a contractor of your abilities. The real formula for success is to begin with a plan, just like you do with any construction project you tackle. Even the most simple construction projects usually start with at least a napkin drawing at the local coffee shop. The questions below will help you determine a plan. Even if you have been in business for twenty years, it is imperative to review your plan on an annual basis. When you ask yourself about your skills, that applies to your personal skills and desires and, as you grow, the skills and desires of the entire crew.

1. What do you want your business to look like?
2. What services do you have the skills and desire to offer? Plumbing_____ Forced air_____ Refrigeration_____ Hydronic

heating_____ Drain cleaning_____ Electrical _____ Design_____ Troubleshooting_____ (Add any others you think of)

3. If you offer a service that requires other skills, do you want to do that? (Sheet metal contractors who install furnaces may also do some architectural metal work.)

4. What will your area be—your local community or a surrounding area of a defined border?

5. What does your area need? Define the services that you can offer to the area.

6. Can you profit from these services?

7. Do you want to offer service work only?

8. Do you want to offer new construction only?

9. Do you want a mix? If so, what do you perceive the mix to be—50/50 or a different matrix? What does your area need?

10. If you are just starting out and want to be both, who do you hire first?

11. If you are a veteran of the industry and looking to expand, what do you want to expand with?

12. What training will you need to meet the plan you have laid out?

13. Where can you get this training?

14. What resources do you have to hire employees?

15. What help do *you* need? (No one has all the skills needed to operate a business without the support systems in play. Do you need a great accountant? Do you need a business coach? Do you need better technical training?) This question makes the list that formulates your weaknesses and helps you to find the answers.

16. Do you have a relationship with suppliers that will profit your endeavors?

17. Can you find suppliers who are willing to be friends and partners? (Most good suppliers want a contractor who is driven to perform to the highest level. Not all suppliers are built to perform that way.)

These questions will get you thinking about large and significant decisions. This is just the beginning of what you need to address.

While the building of a crew is one of the first tasks you will encounter, after you have decided your path, you'll need to address the sustainability of that crew and model. While you may have found a great group or even only one person (if that is your desire), it is also imperative to look at your plan on an annual basis and evaluate if the right folks are still the ones you have.

Several years ago we worked with a business coach at National Comfort Institute (NCI) to create a team evaluation tool that used the Boy Scout creed as the basis. This idea was one that my business coach had, and I wanted to be the beta test group to help with this process.

It was a great experience, and I will explain the concept. Each employee will evaluate using a matrix for every other member of the team, including the owner, based on how they perceive each person operating in each category. We added four traits to the twelve mentioned in the boy scout creed we mentioned earlier, and created a list of sixteen catagories to be used. Each team member used 0 to 10 to rank the other members, as well as themselves, in each category. These were sent via fax or email to our business coach, being careful to keep all submissions confidential. He prepared a report on each person and how they scored, both individually and in comparison to the entire team. This was used to address issues on our team. The business then tallied the scores of each person including myself and we could then address their scores. He also addressed any areas that needed attention and outlined the goals and plans. The business coach complimented their strengths and successes, which provided weight in terms of their raises or bonuses.

The first time we performed this study, it was apparent that two team members needed to leave. We worked to make that change during the next few months. One team member had been with us for more than fifteen years, and at one time I had great confidence in his ability. His attitude had changed, and even with the use of this study to point out weaknesses, he could not be saved.

The outcome was a stronger and more profitable company. By the way, the employee who was laid off was categorized as a reduction in force, and we allowed him to draw unemployment. It was not that he did not pass a drug test or was caught stealing. He just had lost the drive or will to be productive and had developed a victim attitude and could not overcome that.

Building a crew is just like buying a fleet of trucks. If you bought five new trucks of any brand, put fuel in them, and never rotated the tires or greased the chassis or changed the oil, in less than two years you would have a fleet of two-year-old trucks with probably less than fifty thousand miles each that do not run or are not safe to drive.

It is the same with your crew, with the exception that the fleet of trucks would only affect each truck, and your crew members who were no longer team members would have a detrimental effect on the entire crew. While Michael Jackson tried to convince us that "one bad apple don't spoil the whole bunch girl," I believe he was wrong. Left to fester, a member of your staff will destroy your teamwork and create a cancer that may destroy your business.

Proper maintenance is at least as important as, and maybe more important than, proper acquisition. If you do not measure the performance of your crew, you are truly guessing, which leads to false information. Truth will set free any situation and should be held as a very important matrix and indicator of the success of not only your business but your life.

Build a great crew, but, more importantly, maintain a great crew. Greatness can deteriorate into goodness, and the next step is inadequacy. This applies to any mix of your business—construction only, service only, or any combination of that, as well as any discipline on which you build your business. While my experience is in the mechanical industry, this can apply to anything from medical to retail, as any business can be built to succeed with this plan. A business with a great and sustained crew and leadership with vision and the goal of greatness that never deviates from that goal is the key. Constant monitoring is the path to this, along with the never-ending celebration of excellence.

Our society today tends to celebrate just getting by, and often we see the less-than-productive celebrated. Be careful to not follow this path, which only leads to, at best, a good-enough attitude. That is not very rewarding.

After twenty-seven years in this business and forty-two in the industry, it looks like I knew all of this to begin with, but rest assured that I am sharing with you what I learned from HKU (Hard Knocks University). Although I do not have a doctorate from that institution, I am sure I have paid for one at least two times. Bud Moriarty, the owner of APH Service Company in Denver, said to me when I started, "You have the stuff. When you feel like you want to quit, call me, and I will talk you into staying, because I know it will be worth it." There will be trials and tribulations, but if you build a business, you want it to be worth it. Remember that you must always build the business that you want, and that may be different for everybody, as we all want different things from life.

A business that has a good reputation and is profitable can always change to meet the needs of the owners and the market they serve. The financial goals that you have for yourself and your team can be met and even exceeded with the right dedication.

I've met many young technicians who are in business for themselves. Notice that I did not say "businessmen." I find that many of them have embarked on the dream without a plan and just the ability to perform the actual work. While I believe that the working population of America has built this nation into the great nation that it is, I also know that everyone is not equipped or may not have the desires to deal with the daily operation of a business like this. To build a strong nation we need not only strong individuals but also strong companies to fuel and lead our nation back to a prosperous future.

I hope this chapter has helped you define what you want to be when you grow up and will set you on a path for success in whatever you decide to do.

Training and Discipline

In our ever-changing world, training is a new and necessary evil with which we will have to contend. Why I call it evil is simple. Training is a lot like advertising. A good friend of mine who is a car dealer always says that exactly half of the advertising you do actually works. Tell me which half that is, and I will cease the other half. These are great words to think on and take to heart.

I have watched many companies spend large sums of money on training. For the most part, they send employees to classes on every subject in the book. In the HVAC industry, that can be air flow, combustion, troubleshooting, proper refrigeration practices, and a multitude of items that may or may not work. Here are three common problems that detract from productivity:

1. The employees sent for very technical training are so new that they cannot read a tape measure. If they can, they do not know why they are reading a tape measure. This might sound absurd, but if they have only been with you for a period of less than one year and are new to the industry, they probably lack the ability to understand the technicalities of proper refrigerant charging.

2. The employees are not working in the portion of the company for which this training is relevant. The US Army has a philosophy that to teach an individual something, you have to tell them, tell them again, tell them what you told them, ask them what you told them, and watch to see if they understood it. If they are,

say, working on plumbing or even HVAC rough-in, they may not see a set of gauges or a refrigeration bottle for a year or more. You just flushed your training dollars down the proverbial toilet.

3. Training should always improve productivity. In my early years in this industry, while an apprentice plumber/pipe fitter, we had subjects that appeared to be useless or lacked common sense. There was a book on the use and care of tools. While I was in high school Vocational Industrial Clubs of America auto mechanic regional champion and also participated in the Plymouth troubleshooting contest on a state level, I thought I really did not need this. But do you know the proper way to use a pipe wrench? Do you know which cutting oil to use when threading on a power threading machine? If not, then you need training in that area. If you are a plumber, do you know the difference between a vent stack and a stack vent?

The three problems above all point to the same kind of issue: Did you train on combustion and then send a crew out to install a gas piping job, but the crew did not know which oil to use when threading? I used this as I watched three techs threading pipe one day. They all were cussing the brand-new dyes as they wiped the threads off the pipe. One held a master plumber's license, and the other two had worked for at least five years in the trade (though not licensed). Of course, it was not their fault that the brand-new dyes were bad. The attitude of entitlement that was in the shop was as thick as molasses. When I saw they were using oil meant to loosen rust and not thread, I asked, "Who told you to use this oil?" They all began to point fingers. When we used dark cutting, the threads were perfect, and the dyes worked as designed.

What did it cost? We had three journeyman techs, and a helper or two were there, so use the cost of labor in your company. For the most part, these three had been there for at least forty-five minutes, so plan that out at five employees, or a total of 3.75 man-hours. Thank goodness they did not ruin a set of $200 dyes, but they did destroy at least five feet of pipe. It looked to me like I had just lost a $500 bill in this debacle. If they had received some training on combustion and were not using it, they could not have tested that either.

I have a friend who was one of the best refrigeration service techs in the country. He moved to another community and came back to my little area, as he had a service contract with a customer that was a coal mine to take care of all HVAC and refrigeration for them. They wanted a tall wash bay heated, and he sold them on infrared tube heat. It was a great choice for a shop like that, by the way. He had to install several feet of gas piping to serve the new heaters he had hung and vented. He called me and asked if I would go down and help pipe the job with him. He indicated he had 24 hours of labor for two men bid on this for gas piping. I loaded up my 1965 Ridgid 300 and my hand dyes and met him at the mine site. In about six hours of working we were done.

How was this so? Was he lazy? No. Was he trying rip off his customer? No. Did I have the latest machine money could buy? No. What was the difference? It comes down to having been taught how to gas pipe, as Dan Holohan would say, by the dead men. For those of you who do not know who Dan is, he has written in trade publications about all the old-time guys who knew their trade from experience and training, particularly in the steam and hydronic heat portion of the industry. Those guys are now very old or dead, and I was lucky enough to work with many of the now dead men who taught me how to gas pipe. By the way, we did not really work hard at this and used much less pipe than he bought as well.

Did my training pay off? Absolutely. If your staff could gas pipe a job in less time than you bid, did you have a return on investment of your training dollars? Could you create a larger market, as you are more productive and your price reflects that? Could you sell your time at a higher price, because the actual job took less time than that of any competitor? Think about athletics. Take any sport, from football to baseball to team roping. What makes a great heeler? What makes a great linebacker? In all areas it boils down to two things: proper technique and practice of that technique.

I am not a team roper (though I know some who are), but I have coached youth football, and I love defense. Over the years it has been my pleasure to coach many young boys and watch them grow into high school and then see them play. Two tackling examples come to mind. When attending a professional game, I am always disgusted when a $4 million defensive back tries to knock someone out of bounds instead of making a tackle. I have always taught the concept of "stick, wrap, and drive." When I see a high school athlete who I have coached make a tackle, they rarely miss the tackle and usually come up to me after the game to make sure I saw that tackle. Technique and practice as a fifth-grade Doak Walker youth league player were key to making a habit of tackling in these athletes. Seeing the opposing player with the ball in their area made them take careful aim, place their shoulder in the gut (stick), wrap their arms around the player and not let go (wrap), and pump their legs to run through the player, placing them on top of the pile on the turf (drive). How great would your business be if your staff confronted every job with these habits? We practiced that almost every night for warm-ups. The season lasted about six to eight weeks, with two practices per week or a total of around four hours of practice time, divided among twelve players on a team for total of, say, twenty minutes over the course of the season. Many of those young men played for me for only one year. I am not trying to toot my own horn here. I just want to give you a sense of the actual cost and time needed to train staff on proper procedures and habits. I hope that the coaches those players had after me took the time to make sure they had it down.

I have also seen proper technique and habits result from a lack of discipline. Remember that the word "discipline" comes from "disciple," which means a follower of one greater or, as I like to think, one who is trained in and follows the truth. Let's talk about some of the players I coached who were not so successful in later years. Maybe they did not have the reinforcement from coaches to be responsible. Maybe the entire team was a group of undisciplined and rogue players. Maybe they were outclassed by the competition. It is possible a parent who was ignorant of football practices got in the way.

See the pattern here? In all three cases, it is the coach who is at the pinnacle. The buck stops there. Who is that person in your business? It should be you. If you are not ready to teach proper procedures, make sure your training dollars have a return on investment, and hold your staff accountable. You will be at fault for the missed tackles or profit your team has lost.

How do we change course? In our industry today, we are quickly seeing the retirement and the deaths of those who were trained like I was, so the basics are lost. How many times have you heard an NFL coach of a 2-and-14 team say, "We are going back to basics"? That means blocking, tackling, ball handling, and the fundamentals of the game. I would call that the installation side of our industry. The service side tends to need a greater emphasis on the technical and troubleshooting. Even with that said, those team members need to know how to use the tools and what to look for.

Here are some great examples of the fundamentals:

1. Always use a three-point bite with a pipe wrench.
2. Never use larger than an eight-inch adjustable wrench to set a china toilet.
3. Do not use a screwdriver as a chisel.
4. Wear safety glasses.
5. Wear gloves when handling sheet metal.
6. Keep your tools organized.

Those all sound like common sense items, but I have seen many staff members who have been in a trade for thirty years who do not know how to do any of these. Look at the six items I addressed. Number one will keep proper structure to the pipe being loosened or tightened. Have you ever seen a nipple that was egg shaped, to the point it could not be removed or used? That was caused by improper pipe wrench adjustment. Number two is a favorite of mine and probably not in many books, but you will never tighten a toilet and break it with an eight-inch wrench. You will with a ten-inch, and this is for the individual who has never set toilets and has no reference for how tight to make it. There is no sound as bad as the sickening crack from tightening a toilet too tight.

Have you trained your staff for whom you are charging, say, eighty-five dollars per hour and who are costing you fifty-five dollars, know these fundamentals, and do they practice them? I am addressing you the boss now. Do you want a highly trained staff? Do you know what that means? It is really not an advertising statement; it is a way of life. Do your training dollars have a real return on investment? This is not your stockbroker talking. I guarantee that these concepts will make you more than any stock tip you will ever receive from the very best investment broker in the country.

Here is another observation you will make if you watch other trades and businesses. Have you ever been in a restaurant and noticed a server running back and forth and always forgetting to bring the ketchup? In that same setting may be another who seems to handle twice the tables and never runs or looks panicked. Notice the difference. The calm server probably does not make anywhere near the number of trips back and forth due to organization. When that person brings out an order, they remember to bring the Heinz 57 for my patty melt and do not have to return to get it. If you question them, you will find they have developed a system to remember and prioritize each trip to make the job they do less physical and more productive. Henry Ford figured this out and created the production line. The people in our industry now write articles on prefabrication of systems and how to make a job go more quickly. To date I have not seen anything that touches on organization. When all the tools you have in your truck are in the front seat, *you are either disorganized or lazy.* Sometimes lazy folks are not organized, as they think it is too hard, when, in fact, it makes things easier. I often say I do not mind working, but I am lazy by nature. That means I will strive to find an easier way to do something if I can, and organization is one way to do that.

I had a tech who was installing a commercial system just a block from our shop, and he had to drive by a competitor to get there. The competitor told me one time that he would make at least six turnarounds a day in front of his shop. The tech would hop the curb on the right side of the street and then the left and return to my shop for materials he could not remember from thirty minutes prior. By the way, that truck's front end had to be rebuilt and not from any use other than his. He lacked the organization to leave our shop at eight in the morning and work until noon, with no return for materials, and then to return after lunch and work to day's end. It seems pretty easy to me, not that we all do not forget materials. But he could not focus on the job in an organized manner to get it done without spending at least an extra hour per day returning for a part he needed at the moment. There is never a need to do that. You can teach your employees how to do it, but they will have to perform.

I have sat in meetings where productivity ideas are bantered around, and one that always arises is an item called "pull kits," meaning that we have laid out all the materials for a particular task, like a furnace change-out. The gas connector, the gas cock, the thermostat wire, the other things on the list, and then the leftovers are returned to the shop to be used in another kit. That is one way to forego training with productive people.

Truck inspections will leave you sick to your stomach, as some guys are slobs and others cannot organize. The level of production you see from a tech will show you if they are unorganized slobs or if their organization just looks messy to you. I like the idea of anyone being able to find items in a truck without the secret code in their DNA. This is particularly true with an install crew.

Can we teach efficient movement? Many consultants will tell you they can (and I can as well), but you have to want that for yourself and your company. That takes dedication and discipline. It's easy to talk about and hard to execute. Ask yourself, "Am I willing?"

In order to make the change, you need to take at least four hours of a day or evening and tell yourself, "I know nothing about how to train a staff, so how do I do it?" Then get alone, clear your mind, and look at your staff one at a time. Think about what you have seen them do. Ask yourself if some of the things I have mentioned are problems. Think about each individual's time in the industry and whether they should know this or whether you should teach them that now. Be honest. I am sure you are going to say, "Man, I have wasted a lot of time and money and seen no return from it." Did the three-day class on combustion training make the guy who is piping this remodel more productive? Does he remember any of it? You may have paid for the class, but you also paid the employee to sit there, and you lost three days of productivity while they did. It looks to me like it will take six months of improved production piping remodels to pay for the time and effort you put into the training.

I am not down on combustion training. If anything, I am very high on it. I just use it as an example. I firmly believe that all service techs and your experienced folks in the trenches need this training. However, it is wasted on a guy who has been with you for six months to two years and is working as a helper. If in two years he is not moving toward being a real lead tech, then you have another problem. As long as he is banging tin or piping jobs, the best way to enforce these practices is from the lead tech with whom he is working. And he should receive that from management or foremen.

Teach proper duct sizing with each job installed. After a tech has been with you for two years and is showing signs of becoming a real lead tech in your firm, do you send him to a real air balance class? He will have the field experience to understand what he is seeing and also the interest and dedication to improve his worth to your firm.

Any time that an individual is in a trench, precautions need to be taken to make this safe. Safety is not always a course for being more productive, but it is always profitable in lost productivity and even life. It is an OSHA requirement that in a safe ditch there is a method of entry and exit. In other words, there must be a properly placed ladder. I have witnessed guys with the proper ladder on the truck jump into a ditch and also try to boost themselves out of a ditch. I have always told them to get a ladder. Proper discipline means that they do it every time they enter a ditch, not just when you are there to tell them. After ten years of yelling this, I took a new stand in a meeting one morning. "The next time I see one of you in a ditch without a ladder, you are terminated, no questions asked. I will not speak to you. Just go back to the shop, and write your last paycheck with termination for insubordination." Amazingly that worked, and they did not do that anymore. However, that only worked until we hired new folks and forgot to tell them. Then the old folks forgot to tell them. And then we did not practice that, and we missed tackles. Sound familiar? If so, what is the fix?

Brush your teeth. I presume you brush your teeth, as in this country we are trained early to take care of our oral hygiene. Have you ever not brushed for a day? It makes your teeth feel crusty or slimy, right? Well, if you continued that practice, eventually you would have no teeth. While not getting one new guy on board the first day does not make your teeth slimy, it does begin the cycle.

A company's culture is not built on speeches about how they are great. It is built on the practice of being great—a commitment to doing the job well, with great system performance, at a fair price, with a great profit margin for the company. The individual who never gets a job completed within the time bid and is always behind lacks either motivation or training. If they have a license, you have to believe it is a lack of motivation. If they cannot seem to do the project to the quality for which you ask, and the work is, at best, substandard, then training may be an issue. If the work they can produce is good, then they are not motivated, which is another way of saying they are lazy.

Our society today is full of these types of folks, but all are not that way. Send a tinner to install plumbing, and see how productive they are. Even the best tinner will not be a great (or even good) plumber without some training and guidance. If you have a tinner and his helper or apprentice on a job, setting fixtures, and you are an old-time plumber like I am, take the time to explain that the apprentice should trim sinks while you set toilets. Do not have him watch while you work, as we do not pay spectators. When you go to a concert or a sporting event, you normally pay to go there, correct? Well, why would you pay a guy to watch someone work for his entertainment? You should be charging them. I used to pay $100 per seat for tickets in the south stands at Mile High to watch a Denver Broncos game, and that was preseason and regular season. It cost a lot more for a playoff game. Get that helper working, and if they are not capable, get new helpers. If the lead techs are not capable of running another guy for productivity either, work them alone or get new lead techs. The lead techs may need some training and clear expectations of what you want them to do and why you pay them more than the helper with whom they are working.

Training is not only about the actual work you are doing. It is also about the expectations of your staff regarding how they perform and how they interact with others (staff or customers). It is also a company culture that you are instilling in your staff. What is your culture if you looked at your company from an honest outside view?

In all reality, the training is very important, but it is totally lost if there is no follow-through. Let's just concentrate on discipline. A young tech said to me once, "Sometimes, although I am younger than many of our guys, I feel much more mature." Wow. Does your staff remind you of a kindergarten class? I have watched employees leave the shop to ride fire trucks and not tell anyone. I have seen employees work one supervisor against the other like a spoiled toddler who works their parents. I have seen employees do the exact opposite of what they were told, with no consequence. What will that do to the staff? Nothing good, I can guarantee you.

I have a cute little niece who I dearly love. When she was about a year old, I would volunteer to take her at any family function. I would feed her the bottle so her mother could eat. While I fed her I would sing to her. It was special to me and I hope to her as well. This little girl, who is now about six, has a linebacker, spit-in-your-eye attitude. Often when we are out she acts like something I do not want to claim. One night in particular she was especially difficult. Just before we were about to leave, she asked my wife for some gum. My response was "No!" My wife was going to give her a piece from her purse, and I explained that I would put her over my knee as well if she did. Then I explained to my niece that she did not get a reward for being a pain. Her mom looked at me with thanks in her eyes, and we left without any gum. About a week later, we were out again and she was a delight. At the end of the meal, she asked me if she could have some gum. I said yes. To this day she knows that if I am there, I control the gum, and her actions control her getting any gum. I cannot say what happens when I am not there, but the sure thing is when I am, she acts differently, or no gum is granted.

What has she learned? Discipline! Your staff are a bunch of six-year-old nieces. If you keep giving them gum and praising when they act like brats, you are setting the company culture. Like Arnold in *Kindergarten Cop,* you are now the owner of Kindergarten Mechanical.

When a master plumber plays the supervision one against the other to get their way, *do not give them any gum.* Better yet, respect those who are not this way. Rid yourself of this soul-sucking problem. When you fail to hold them accountable, you show that you do not understand how to operate a business, or you are afraid of them. Decide today which it is, and either pull on your big-boy pants and take charge, or hire someone who can do it for you. Get yourself some training to allow you to be the boss and the person who sets the culture for your company.

I have had many employees who were separated from this company for one reason or the other. Most of the time they have thanked me for helping them to grow up. *Do not allow childish behavior to rule your domain.* If you are a child yourself, then I can only say *grow up* or fail.

These are tough words, and I know you will not like hearing them, but please do not think I am telling you anything I have not had to learn myself from HKU (Hard Knocks University). Campuses are in every corner of the country. If I can save you one of the painful lessons I learned the hard way by writing this down, then it is all worth it.

You, as an owner or manager, are responsible for seeing a return on investment for your training dollars. That means you must do the following:

1. Determine who needs what.
2. Train for productivity, not just knowledge.
3. Test to be sure any of this stuck.
4. Repeat the subject in a practice situation to ensure habit building.
5. Train in fundamentals for each trade and the basics that apply to all you do.
6. Build a culture where the lead techs also train the newcomers in that culture.
7. When someone acts like a toddler, treat them as such (in other words, discipline them).
8. If they do not change, *remove the problems!*

The Art of Negotiation

After you have been in this business for about thirty minutes, you may enter into your first negotiation. As a matter of fact, you may have started this as young as three or four, when you first wanted to do something of which your mother or father did not approve. Remember back to your childhood. If you had a parent or grandparent or other adult authority figure, you probably began to negotiate to get the item you desired. At that time your only thought was "I want what I want," and you did not care about the future, the dangers, or the historic outcome of your actions. With adulthood comes the responsibility of caring for the future of your actions. You want your decisions to be positive and a possible win-win for all involved. There are times when it can only be a win for one of the parties involved, but that is partially dependent on the point of view. It is also dependent on your world point of view.

Your first negotiation could be your first service call or new construction job or first conversation with a supplier of materials. Either way, you have to enter these with a positive mind-set that will pave the way for future relationships that are profitable for both parties. Remember that if only one finds it enjoyable, it is case of one party taking advantage of another and that usually ends in disgust.

We can take advantage of the land much as the original strip mines did and now we know better. We can take advantage of our employees by paying far below what they are worth and not valuing their efforts. We may taken advantage of our former employers but not producing an honest day's work for an honest day's pay. We can be taken advantage of by the customer that only wants to hire you because you are the cheapest and does not care if you can sustain your business as long as they get your quality for a bargain price and if you do the installation well they need not worry about the future of your business as they have what they want.

Negotiation is at every turn of your future. *American Pickers* is a show on the History Channel where people travel around the country and buy antiques and high-quality items that can be resold for a profit. I watched Mike and Frank go from one town to the next. Danielle set them up with picks on the phone. They sometimes encountered the seller who really understood what the item was worth in a high-end retail shop. That was the price they wanted for it in a ramshackle barn that had fifty years of dust and chicken droppings on it. They rarely bought that item, as the owner thought all his junk was gold and anyone else's junk was junk. Then they went to a location where the owner had something that was very valuable and offered it to Mike or Frank for ten cents on the dollar of a wholesale price. Mike and Frank many times on this show have said, "I think you are light on that. I will give you four times that amount." Of course, they looked like real stand-up guys. I thought they were, but they still had won the negotiation game, as the item was moved to a more profitable position, and the former owner received more than they ever thought it was worth.

I had a similar project with only two or three years under my belt when I presented a bid to a motel owner for a new domestic hot water heating system. After I presented my bid he said, "I know what all this equipment costs and what I figured I could spend, and I want you to make a fair profit, so I will pay this much more than your bid for this project." Wow. I was surprised, but I liked the exchange. He understood that if I did not make a profit that allowed me to grow the business, he was affecting himself, me, and our community in a negative way. What a great worldview.

We installed the system, and not only did we make a profit, but we made a relationship that lasted for many years. He helped to grow the business by recommending us to his friends and other contacts who needed our style of service. What a great experience.

You may run into a supplier who only wants you to buy from them to be a profit center for their business and offer no service. That is a relationship that cannot be sustained. While there are times you may help yourself in buying from them, they will never be profitable to you as a contractor. Remember that "profitable" is not just about making money. Relationships can be profitable as well. Folks help you when you help them, and that is a great way to do business.

You will negotiate with employees many times, and this is where most contractors fall short. Also when you are asked to perform work for folks you regard as friends many times negotiations fall short. You may have began learning what it takes to make your business sustainable and feel that you cannot charge a fair price for your service when working for them. They also may now expect more work for less money since they were some of the folks that told you to do this for yourself. Often when you now need to make an honest profit, you quote them a price. They now think you are trying to get to them, but weren't they the ones who gave you this idea? They don't sound like friends to me. By the way, you are now the boss, and it is your responsibility to make an honest profit so that you can pay an honest wage.

I have seen contractors who wanted to hire a true journeyman installer for less than twelve dollars per hour, or about what is considered starvation wages. We bring our problems on ourselves when we think we can do this. If we need help, we should know what our market wage is and be willing to (1) charge what we need to bring the profit to pay our help fair and (2) fight the greed that would make us not share in the profit with our employees. You are only as strong as your weakest link, and if you believe a talented individual would stay with you and perform quality work for half of the market wage, then I have to label you as a fool. That is not a sustainable mind-set and is not a win-win for anyone.

I do not believe you have won if one of the parties in the negotiation feels unfairly compensated. That is not a negotiation; it is a travesty. You should receive the value all high-quality items command. A laborer is worthy of his hire. Do not muzzle the ox that treads the grain. If you think I am out of line here, let's shed some light on this train of thought. Your business is a laborer, and you and all your staff are worthy of their hire, right? If someone thinks that you are not, you cannot win with that party. If you do not think you are, you should stop thinking about being in business this minute. If you have any self-esteem or pride and cannot see that you are worth your hire, then not only will you damage yourself in business, but you will damage the market and the industry. Once you decide that the industry really is comprised of "lightning wranglers," "weather controllers," and "protectors of the health of the nation," then you are ready to be in business. That is the entry-level thinking you need to establish an iconic business that meets the needs of the customers, community, and employees.

I hope this discussion has set your mind in motion and that you are thinking about negotiation in a positive light. I hope as we progress, you will make great strides in your skills and your ethics as a negotiator. Let's move on to what to look for as you hire employees and draw in customers.

In my forty-two years of experience in this industry, I have had many unique experiences. I have been contacted by individuals who attempted to make me work for them when I knew either they were using me as a last resort or they believed they could take advantage of my experience and get a Cadillac job for a Volkswagen price. (That lost something in the passage of time, as the Volkswagen is no longer the inexpensive car it once was.) Many have heard great reviews but do not want a relationship with me as a contractor. They only want me to quote a lower price, do it faster, or fix the mess someone else made for a bargain price. I know that they'd be taking advantage of me, and I do not desire that. So I normally refuse, and if I do take it on, it is at a premium price.

Think about this. A Lexus is nothing more than a Toyota with a different level of trim, a fancier showroom, and a much higher price. The same holds true for a Chevrolet to a Cadillac or a Ford to a Lincoln. The same engine and drivetrain are in both sides of those three examples, and often they share frames and some body panels. Why do we pay more? The quality is not a lot greater, but the experience may be. The same corporations produce both sides of all of the examples, and you can do that as well.

You can be profitable with a low-income housing project and with a $4 million mansion in a resort area. The actual pipe and ductwork or wiring you use will be the same for both projects, and the actual labor mind-set is also the same. A major factor is where and how you negotiate. Part of that is creating the atmosphere of quality and the feeling of confidence that allows you to upsell. Notice I did not say "arrogance," as no one likes to be treated with that, but there is an air of confidence that we all seek when we are negotiating any purchase or operation.

I am reminded of the Charlie Daniels song "The Devil Went Down to Georgia." Here is a situation with Satan looking to steal a soul. He runs into a confident individual who is his match. The fiddler ends the competition with "I told you once, you SOB, I am the best there's ever been." That has a sound of arrogance, but he did not state that with the attitude until he proved his ability. I often joke with general contractors that they build sheds and warehouses and we make them homes when they have plumbing and heating. They always laugh, but we have proven our point many times, as we have kept them out of the fire with our services.

Are you really as good as you think you are? Do others have the same opinion of you? Do you rub it in people's faces? The first two questions are answered by a vote of the dollar bill, as you are hired to perform your craft. The third is a testament to your character. If the answer is yes, you do not have any character. If the answer to the first two is yes, then you have the beginning of a great platform for negotiation.

As you progress and grow, you will find that you often will land jobs due to reputation. If not priced for profit, you will have done yourself a disservice. If you are priced too high, you will eventually get a bad reputation for that as well. Just as Mike and Frank know what the item is worth, you should know what your service is worth as well and be willing to negotiate from a win-win position of knowledge and strength. Everyone is a winner with this attitude, and you will sleep at night with confidence, knowing that you are providing a profitable and needed service to your area.

Hopefully your mind is in line with the responsibility and character you need to move forward. Now let's talk about different red flags and green lights you will encounter. The first red flag is the customer or other party who wants to be the ultimate winner. For the sake of this discussion I will adopt the belief that if you have read this far, you have made the adjustment in your thinking, and you now have the character to succeed and to create relationships.

This new customer who comes to you with the idea that they can get this work for your cost will never be profitable to you. There's no need to negotiate with them, but it is good to inform them of the facts. They will probably leave, buy somewhere else, and always say they got a great deal, which will prove to be untrue. I am sure that eventually the work they either did themselves or hired an outsider to perform will be substandard and often dangerous. I recommend developing a real nose for smelling this out. Keep your encounter brief and to the point. Politely explain that you cannot help them, and be sincere with your attitude. There is no reason to be ugly or nasty about it. Just as Paul Simon says, "get yourself free."

I usually indicate that we cannot take on another project at this time, and that is always the truth. I have found it better to not say "I do not want to work for you" and rather just let them know that I cannot take on another project at this time, as we will disappoint you with our service. I've always believed it is better to not get involved with a perceived problem than to take it on and find yourself stuck in the tar baby and being sucked in to a situation that is not rewarding or profitable.

Having said all of that, you will continue to advertise and attempt to attract new customers, as long as you are in business. They will usually be from a service call background. You have very little exposure to harm with this type of job, as you will not tie up thousands of dollars in materials or equipment and very little labor costs, so it is always easier to remove yourself from that relationship. I am not saying to stop looking for new customers, but I am saying that you may find that all of them do not desire the type of service you have decided to offer.

Let's talk about the customers who need your service and are willing to pay for it. They come to you with an attitude of "I need this done" and "please help me." That is the most enjoyable beginning to a relationship and negotiation you will ever experience. With character, you can meet and exceed these folks' needs and desires and make a fair profit as well. A fair profit is based on your cost of business, not the going rate in your area. That being said, I often find that we can perform at a higher level for the same cost and even lower than some of our competition. John Q. Public comes to you and needs a system for his home. He hasn't talked to everyone around, and he says you are the best. This type of customer usually is prepared to use your expertise in your craft, and that is a great experience. Be sure not to take advantage of others, but provide a great product at a fair price.

Several years ago in Steamboat Springs, a concrete contractor who wanted to build a nice but not extravagant house in Steamboat called and wanted a price on HVAC that included two furnaces and cooling systems. The total size of the house was about two thousand square feet up and down, with a planned system for the upstairs and one for the downstairs. It was a pretty simple request, but at the time we were very busy. I did not know him, so I kindly declined the project. He then told me that he did not really want me to bid on it but rather just do it, as he could only get one contractor to give him a price, and it was over $50,000 for the two systems. That was quite a lot of money. He was a victim of a very busy building market and someone who was out to take advantage of the market. I am sure that the systems that were installed were not good quality, and I am not talking about the equipment used.

We have followed many contractors and rectified systems that were undersized or not commissioned and were never able to properly heat or cool the spaces they served. We have also had to make plumbing repairs to systems that were poorly installed, at best, and I am always amazed at the level of service some individuals provide. While I want to encourage you to make a fair profit and be able to afford the things you have worked hard for, I cannot condone actions that do not provide service to the level of the profit you receive.

Most of what we have discussed so far will address your character and perception. Now we need to prepare for proper negotiations. You are looking at a project that is a planning nightmare and also is many miles from your home base. While I have always been good at naming a price, I recently looked at a house that is an hour and a half from the shop one way, and the house has nine HVAC systems in it with lots of ductwork. We actually are doing this job on a time and materials basis, as I could not figure how to fairly price all the travel we would have to pay for. It has been a great job and led to a good relationship with the owner and all the properties that are around this house. I would venture that this house will cost somewhere in the $25 million range, and I would guess that our higher estimate due to travel would not be a problem.

Another contractor had quoted a price on this house. When he was questioned, without hesitation he verbally reduced his price by around 40 percent. What do you think he was doing?

We have built our business on the idea that if we all have a feeling of a win, then we have made a profit. Our bank account shows that to be true not only with the profits from the original job but with the ongoing relationship we have established with many important clients. They keep calling and putting money in our account while we take care of their plumbing and HVAC issues or help them with new projects.

You will also have additional negotiations with employees. These are some of the most stressful relationships that you will have. You must hire individuals at a level at which they can perform. You are also looking to build long-term relationships with them. There may come a time when you have to make a move with an employee. Unlike negotiating with customers or other contractors and suppliers, this one will be crucial to your survival. While I am always willing to pay what they are worth, you must always judge if they are worth what you are paying. This is less a matter for conjecture and more a matter of compliance. The individuals who you hire will be working with your customers when you are not there. Will they hold to your standard? Will they leave a good impression? When you hire, you must not tie yourself to a situation that leaves you no escape.

When one job is done, you can easily make the choice to not take on another contract if this one has proven to be problematic. Employees may start out doing well and later become a problem, and that leaves you with no recourse that is pleasant. I always hold to the belief that one problem individual should not be allowed to create an environment of total discourse in a company. Sometimes you can correct or negotiate a change in behavior, and most times you cannot.

While I am a believer in win-win situations, there are times when the individual will be happier if not involved with the organization any longer, and I am sure that the organization is happier without that individual. The end of negotiations, even when started with a win-win attitude, must always end with what is best for your business. This is never as important as it is with employees.

"The good of the many far outweigh the good of the few or the one," Mr. Spock told Captain Kirk, as he had given his life to save the ship and exposed himself to deadly radiation that led to his death. This comes into play with employees even more than customers, and there are times when the only feasible outcome is a separation of the employee and the company. While this does not sound like a negotiation, it really is and will be key to your success.

Your character should lead you to offer a fair wage and a decent job to every individual you hire. The wage should be in keeping with the skills that an individual presents and that will expect a level of character from the employee, who provides a fair day's work for that wage. When you look in the mirror, if you cannot say you have kept your end of the bargain, then I have to condemn you for this mistake. However, just because you are doing the right thing does not mean that all the folks you encounter are as well. Never be afraid to keep a crew of individuals who hold true to their side of the equation. The quickest way to destroy that is to allow individuals to hang around who do not believe in the employee side of that equation.

Negotiation depends on skills in communication, but the highest level of skill will never replace the proper attitude and character. You really do "wrangle lightning," "control the weather," and "protect the health of the nation." But that does not give you a pass to be a prima donna or a used car salesman. You have a responsibility to perform your craft to the best of your ability and make a fair profit, but you also have a responsibility to be of good character and above reproach. Good negotiation comes from the correct foundation of confidence and compassion and will always create win-win situations when it does.

How to Fire a Customer and How to Make Good Ones

In any business you will encounter customers who take up more time and effort than they provide. There are four types of customers, ranging from A to D. The A customer is your best chance to make a fair profit and have a happy life. B customers are good and mostly loyal, but you will lose them only if you make major errors. C customers are the "first price" shoppers and will never be totally loyal. Then D customers are those who feel that you have taken the Hippocratic oath of plumbing and heating, and you have to meet their needs just because you are in business. You may find them to be ones you try to serve at an entry-level basis, but they will never result in a profit, and you will be lucky if you break even serving them. They do not present a happy vibe to your existence, and you are better off without them, no matter how big the area you serve.

John is the owner of a Chinese restaurant. He bought the business from a former owner and a fairly good B customer. He is demanding and always looks over the tech's shoulder while working, making comments that he will not pay if the tech did not fix the problem and complaining that "he was not there five minutes and you charged me an hour?" The techs hated to go there to work but felt it was their duty to serve him, as this was our policy. While I was on a conference call he came in and confronted the front office with those types of comments for several minutes, which consumed time for which we could not bill.

Being a dutiful employee, Linda tried to diffuse the situation and was presented with "You give me discount?" to which she answered, "No, we were there, and we did our job, and you will have to pay, as we would if we ordered egg rolls." He protested and left.

After my call ended, I came out of my office and found the staff discussing the situation. A plumbing tech who hated to go there was present for the whole ordeal. I asked, "Do you guys like going there?" All replied no, and I knew this was not a profitable customer. Linda gave me the invoices, and I called the customer and simply asked about the discount he wanted. I told him we would offer a 10 percent discount on the total bill if paid by the following Monday, as this was late Friday afternoon. Of course, after listening to much banter in another language, he was quick to ask if we could take the card over the phone. We did and were paid for all work completed, less the discount. They are now on the no-serve list, and we will not be caught there again, as long as John owns the business. I was very pleasant and helpful on the phone and did not address the issue of not returning, as it really makes no difference in the discussion of getting paid.

A servant-minded contractor often will find that they are in a one-way relationship with a customer who will never result in profits and will prove to take time that could be spent and billed to an A or B customer, making them and you happy, comfortable, and profitable. Making a fair profit and helping folks improve their life is our goal. It is wrong and, dare I say, a sin to allow a customer like John to rob us and the other customers of that goal. However, never fire a customer if they owe you money.

Always get the money that you can, and do so with a smile on your face. Ridding yourself of a problem should make you happy. A small discount is the price you pay to remove yourself from a bad situation, and 10 percent is a small price. You may be faced with a repentant customer if you are in a small town like I am, but hold to your guns. I have found that these customers have not changed but really are just desperate to have their immediate needs met.

Taking this a small step further, I have always had the policy that if I did not feel right about taking on a customer, it is better to not do it. I have been known to live by the motto "I never didn't get a job that hurt me any."

In the course of twenty-seven years in business, I have had many opportunities to form a customer relationship with a new general contractor or a new service client. It is always good to know with whom you are entering into a relationship. In the case of a service client, you will usually find out with one or two jobs whether it is good to enter into a long-term working relationship with them. That is one of the reasons we should reserve the right to not renew a service agreement. I would characterize this as a "going steady" relationship. With a service client, you may find you need to break up, or you may find a friend for life who will not only respect your work and efforts but also help to promote those as you go through life. If you do not bid on new construction, you will find that offering a bid to everyone you call is seldom productive. It is much more profitable to build relationships with general contractors who use you for all the work they do and depend on your company for its contribution to each project. I am always suspicious of the new guy looking for a cheap price and heard you were that guy. It is better for them to say, "The reason I got this contract is that I promised them you would do the mechanical." It is a great feeling to build that reputation.

In the economic downturn around 2009, we were hustling to keep ahead. While we were profitable, it was much more work than I had ever experienced. A good customer asked me to bid on a custom home in Steamboat Springs that had solar and several other upscale options to consider. He was not the low bidder, and I had not bid on this job with anyone else. I had never worked with the successful general contractor, and three to four weeks after the bid was due, he called me to ask for my numbers. It seems he had told everyone in Steamboat Springs that one company had the job but never communicated that to them. When he finally called, they had decided to close up shop, seek other means of support, and refused the job. This left him in a scramble to find a mechanical contractor, and he called us for our price on the job.

I had already prepared a price, so the work was done. I just needed to send it to him with his name on the bid. I was not comfortable with him to begin with, as I had heard how he had communicated with a firm that had worked for him many times before, so I knew he was not a relationship builder. I sent him our number, and a day later he called to express that my deduction for the solar portion of the job, if it were deleted, was lower than the guys he had not called back. He asked that I check that out and get back with him, as my numbers were close to the ones he had used to prepare his budget. He called me on my cell phone while I was on another project and working to lay out that project to begin the installation.

This call created in me what I call a gut check. I really did not care what the other guy's deduction was. Here we were, already negotiating price changes, when we had not even met face-to-face. The feeling that I usually describe as an ache in my gut prompted me to call him back and decline to do the job.

The general contractor for whom I had prepared the numbers was shocked that I would turn down so much work. How could I afford to do that? The policy I have lived by is when I take on a new construction project like this, I am determined to complete it, no matter what we encounter. We were already on the rocks, so it was better to decline and not get involved. That has worked well for me, and every time I have violated the gut check, it has been detrimental to our outcome and bottom line.

I actually learned this from a furnace bid I presented in my first four years of operation. A couple called and wanted to install a gas forced air furnace in a slab-on-grade house that was all electric. I presented a price and did not hear from them again, and I thought the work was completed by another contractor. I felt that I had dodged the bullet on that one. A year later, they called back and wanted to revisit the furnace. They had decided to go with our local gas utility company, which quoted them a low and unreasonable rate for a furnace, but they had delayed the decision for a year. In that year, the company had sold, and they no longer performed installation or service past the meter. They refused to contract the job.

I received the call, and when I arrived they informed me that the utility company had quoted a much lower price than ours. They wanted that price but our installation. I explained that I could not install it like I had planned for that price, and we settled on the ductwork being exposed in the living room, which had a vaulted ceiling, with them installing a soffit at a later date. That was all great with them until the installation was complete. Then we had a problem. They did not like the ductwork there, and they wanted to contest our work, even though all had been inspected and permitted. They were impossible to deal with.

They called another contractor, who told them he could put the ductwork in the attic for around $3,000, which was about the amount that the utility company had priced them below my first price. I settled with them, and in our price we had roughed in a gas line to the newly possible electric range. I assured them that I would take care of the warranty for the furnace, but with the signed agreement we were through with discussing any more. Five weeks later they called and wanted us to come out and hook up the new range, as they needed it that day. They were amazed when I refused. To my surprise, I had to explain to them that I was not going to do any other work for them ever again. They could not understand why I felt this way, and I had to chalk this up as a time I should have said no before I was in this deep. Sometimes "Just say no" is not for drugs only.

We still advertise and look for new clients all the time. We have operated in a town of around fifteen thousand for twenty-seven years and rarely travel more than forty miles for projects (and only for large construction projects then). We do not really market service work in those other areas. Having experienced this in such a small place, I can only presume that the larger your population base is, the easier it is to avoid the D customer. I have likened this to the dating concept. No matter how great the person looks, it is better to get to know them before you marry them. That too-good-to-be-true situation is almost always really too good to be true. Even if it is with a customer with whom you have a great relationship, you can always temper your excitement by looking at your company's ability to do the job, create a happy customer, make a profit, and not tie yourself to a project that will prove to devastate your company and personal well-being. I sum this up with Clint Eastwood's immortal words: "A man's got to know his limitations."

A general contractor with whom we have performed many jobs wanted to look at a job that was about twenty miles away from our office and in another county. He took me, a flooring contractor who is a friend and a property partner of mine, and an electrical contractor to look at this property. This job was a *dog,* and we looked the house over with no prints or specs to use and just the owner telling us all he wanted. The owner then began to tell us of his experiences in another state, how he was "ripped off," and the ridiculous prices that other contractors had quoted for work. All of this conversation was after he talked about all the things that were needed here. He wanted hardwood floors on a slab that was cracked and not level and had many other problems. He wanted the best boilers and radiant floors, if possible, and new windows in a house that was partially log, and the three bottom courses of logs were rotted and had to be replaced. He set unreal expectations for this project, including the cost he was willing to pay to resolve all the issues.

I listened to this guy for about an hour and a half and realized these were precious seconds that I would never get back. We got back into the truck, and I announced that we would not be doing that job. Even if it cost our relationship with this general contractor, we would not provide any work or pricing. At this time, the other contractors were worried about how much work they had and believed they needed more than what was on their schedules. I still held my ground and did not involve myself with this dog of a project that would lead to certain financial distress and consume valuable resources of my company.

The other guys did the job with a different mechanical contractor. Just as I had thought, they ended up with "I will furnish all the materials, and you just provide the labor." Being in this business for this amount of time has taught me that I need to run from those projects, as I cannot cover the cost of business with substandard materials and the junk that folks think are good items. They usually have defects, which I am expected to fix, and warranty, when I did not furnish them. This kind of customer will ask for your labor and materials to be separated so they can buy the materials elsewhere for less than you quoted. Never quote them anything but your cost for the materials if you want to do this. It is best to just dismiss this project and find a better place to spend your time. *Never be afraid to just say no to a project that looks like a problem, because it probably is.*

Make sure you have a policy in place (and all employees know about it) to keep from getting involved with a project like this or one for a former customer who was a problem and did not pay or was impossible to deal with. A customer whom we had placed on the no-service list had moved to another city and called with a boiler problem. The customer service representative (which in our small company was also our secretary) took the call and knew full well that this customer was on this list. She dispatched a tech who was more suited for forced air and refrigeration to the job. This young tech was diligent and focused on getting the job done. He waded into this project and ran into multiple complications at this job site. The new boiler was warranted, and now we were up to our eyes in a project for which I knew we would have a hard time getting paid. To this day, I believe that the secretary took the call out of spite, and she is no longer here.

We are still getting paid for this project, as the customer was trying to sell the unit and did not have the money to pay or the ability to finance the job due to a poor credit rating. This was a customer with whom we did not formally make the break, as they were moving out of town, and that should have handled the problem. We could have politely declined the job based on our present workload, and our competitor would now be strapped, trying to get their money. The customer service representative knew but choose to ignore our policy and leave us exposed to this damage. We had a tech tied up doing the job and lost the opportunity for profit with another project. To top off the pain, we did not get paid in a timely manner.

Most of your jobs will be a positive and profitable experience. But you must protect yourself from the negative jobs and rid yourself of that danger. Watch your staff to be sure they realize this hurts not only the company but the very cash flow lifeblood that pays their wages.

What will make you want to quit this business and either work for someone else of go into a new field will probably be related to an individual who works for you or a very difficult customer. Sometimes you hit a string of customers who think they own you. It is a little like Brer Rabbit and the Tar-Baby. The more he fought to escape, the more entangled he became. It will probably not be government regulation, taxes, products, or the hours that finally get to you; it will be the difficult people—the employee who continues to make errors that are like death by a thousand cuts, or the customer who you keep trying to make happy but they would complain if you paid them to show up to their house and fix their furnace. You keep trying and never succeed with making any of them happy, and it is devastating.

Never allow yourself to become one of those people, no matter how hard life gets. It is too short and not worth it. And keep a short account of those folks who suck your energy dry. The employee who refuses to pull their weight needs to be removed. I am not talking about the person who has a bad day or a difficult situation in their life. I am talking about the person who is a disruption wherever they go and creates drama and tension, robbing you of energy and productivity. The same holds true for the customer who creates the same energy, robbing relationships and being a problem as you try to deal with them. If you have performed to the best of your ability and corrected the mistakes you may have made and they still are difficult and probably not paying, then cut your ties and improve your life.

I have been able to do this in a town of fifteen thousand people and even cut ties with general contractors for whom we plumbed and heated up to forty or fifty homes, and I am still in business. If I can do it and you are in a community of a hundred thousand, so can you. Actually it should be easier for you than it was for me.

I heard a saying the other day: "It is time to stop crossing oceans for those who will not step across a puddle for you." That rang true to me. I realize that you cannot keep your energy up, so you can perform for the folks who appreciate it, whether they are customers or employees, unless you look at all relationships in this manner. I am not saying that there will not be times you feel that you are not getting the respect that you deserve, but also there are times that you work all day for individuals who are only using you. That can be draining on resources, including cash and patience and even the patience of your employees. All relationships have to start with a servant attitude, but there will be a time when that may have to end for the good of yourself and the business.

I have always believed that a business that has a servant attitude will provide the better rewards but we have to be careful to not allow overbearing individual to control our lives, many others suffer from their involvement in our business. Our employees and good customers are at risk of harm if we allow them to hold us hostage.

In the twenty-seven years that I was in business, I developed a great relationship with a restaurant owner who had a chain of Village Inns all over Colorado. While we really only serviced the one in Craig, we also worked on at least four other locations, as far away as two hundred miles. We did not have to bid on the job, just budget it, and they were happy to pay for our lodging while we were there. In the beginning of this business, we also had the HVAC contract at a mine south of Craig that had us work on bulldozer AC and all types of things. This was a remnant of the business I bought to get started. Often they would call, and I would leave Craig for the forty-five-minute drive to the location, only to be told that they had to put that back in service, as they did not know when I would make it. I usually called them to let them know I was leaving, and rarely did I not show up in a two-hour window from the time they called. I was set to assume all of their work eventually, but at this time I and the other business shared them, and I did most of the work by then.

One Friday I was leaving to meet a supplier in Rifle to get a commercial water heater for the local Village Inn. Theirs was leaking, and without a water heater, they are shut down. While at home preparing to leave, the phone rang. It was that mine with a bulldozer down. They had several extra units that they could employ, but this one was down now, and I needed to be there. I explained that I could not be there until Saturday, but if they could wait, I would work late and install this water heater. The response was "You are really putting us in a bind, as we need you now." Remember I said we went there several times, to no avail? And while I charged them for the trip, I left someone who needed me high and dry. I went to the water heater and later to the mine. I called the individual who had hired another tech and let him keep that mine, and we amended our agreement. It was the best decision I made in the first five years. I gave up what looked to be a great cash flow customer but was really a tar baby that would rival Brer Rabbit's, and went on to build a business that has been profitable and always busy. We also diversified our client base and made a business that was not focused on only one large client which is closer to being an employee of that client that a business.

We have performed work for them since but not regularly. We work at another mine quite often, and they are a partner, not a dictator of our business and our profit. It is a much better relationship. When asked to do a video presentation for our website, our mine customer was more than happy to. Actually they gave the best testimony of all the customers we asked to do so. They have a different way of doing business, and it is in line with our philosophy, so it is a joy to work with them on any project they bring to us.

In all reality, I guess I have been firing customers since day one, as I realize that they are not worth the profit that they dangle in front of me. Gross revenue is not profit. You can go broke with high gross revenues that take all your time to build profitable, enjoyable, and lasting relationships.

Bidding on Construction Projects

The move to being a contractor may present the opportunity to bid on projects larger than simple furnace replacements and other service-related projects. Many do not want to deal with this pressure, so they refuse to bid on this type of project. Due to the location in which we operated, it was imperative that we performed construction projects. A large portion of our work was due to this in the early to middle years. Today we still bid on projects quite often both in our local town and in Steamboat Springs, which is forty miles away.

The following outline is based on a project on which we bid recently for the local fire department. This is a metal building with several systems included in it. The first step is to break down the building into bite-size pieces and then tackle them one at a time. Remember that the way to eat an elephant is one bite at a time. If you have never bid on a project like this, it will look overwhelming in the beginning. After a few years, you can roll out the prints and say, "Fifty thousand dollars." You will be surprised at how you can develop this ability. That being said, never let that make you presume and not figure the job!

I like to begin with the ground up. Since we do plumbing as well, we will start there. All buildings will have some underground plumbing. This building had trench drains to install and sand oil interceptors, as well as the waste for toilets and other plumbing fixtures. I use a pricing sheet. If you do not have a program for this, that is from NEBS, and it is product #235. On that sheet I address the job name, date, name of the person who priced the job, and description of the actual work. In this case, the work was underground plumbing and trench drains. After I read through the prints and specifications, I determined what type of materials were specified and the practices needed to complete the job. Often I have priced a job as drawn. When L copper was specified and the price was too high, we installed PEX underground and saved a lot of labor and materials to install in this manner. Remember that your beginning price needs to be as drawn and specified, even if you know a better way. Often I have saved tens to hundreds of thousands of dollars and raised my profit margin in the job.

Measure from the print the amount of underground waste line that is to be installed and the length of the trench drain. You can get a pricing book that will give you the national average of labor for all plumbing and heating functions, and you will count the fittings and compile a list of those on your pricing sheet. Call suppliers, secure pricing for the materials, and place that price under one of the columns. Items like sand/oil interceptors will have to be searched out in your area. I have a list of suppliers for all types of odd things, and I use the internet for searching these out. As you progress, and if you use the national labor factors, you will provide the labor needed to install the job. Then all you have to do is multiply the hours by your hourly rate. This may not be your service rate, as you will likely have some apprentice or laborer who is not a fully skilled tech (or two) on the job to provide what we call a helper to install the job. You can use the actual count of fittings, or I tend to budget these on a small job like this as a percentage of the cost of the total developed pipe that I have figured. I tend to express these costs as our cost of materials and then figure my labor as an additional item so we can track that as the job progresses. Most of the time I include all waste and vent through the roof on this sheet, unless the job is split into multiple prices. That is sheet #1.

After I have looked at underground waste lines, I usually work on the water lines next and perform the same functions by measuring the length of piping needed and determining if it is insulated and how it is hung or installed. Again you can use a pricing manual and estimate each fitting you think will be needed. Or with a job as small as this, you can use the percentage factor. You must include insulation on the water piping, if specified, and hangers are another item to be considered. Water piping will include the piping to the stop on each fixture, but not including the stop, and to any valves needed for this installation. Do not forget meters and backflow preventers if they are specified. If not, I do not include them, as that will increase your price. If the specifications list the items to be priced, then that is what you price. Make a note, however, that this is by plans and specifications in your bidding documents so you do not get stuck with something on which you did not bid. This created sheet #2.

Plumbing fixtures are next, with a bid from our suppliers on the fixture specified or with our specification list being priced. This can be by actual fixture or a predetermined budget price of each fixture if you want it that way. With three toilets at $237.69, the total will create the beginning of the list. Then we look at lavatories, faucets, showers, valves, sinks, tubs, and any other fixtures on the drawing. The labor for this will be to set the fixtures and include a cost for P-traps, bowl waxes, supplies, stops, and escutcheons—in other words, all trim pieces. If there is a water heater, which there usually is, that heater and all piping and valves to that heater are in this pricing sheet. This includes an allowance for venting the water heater, but usually the price for gas piping is an additional sheet. This is sheet #3. The service lines often are not part of our scope of work. We bid on them on an additional sheet, but we only mention them here, as normally our prices are figured to five feet outside of the building. We still run many sewer and water service lines but not on every project.

Gas piping is usually included in the plumbing section of a bid. Even if you perform all aspects of the mechanical work, the bid may call for a plumbing number and an HVAC number. You need to ask where to put this number and then put it there. Job one for this is to size the line, if not specified, and often it is not. Even if it is, check that the engineer sized it properly.

It costs very little to upsize a line when installing, and it can be a real problem to retrofit one when it is discovered that you cannot keep all equipment running because the gas line is too small. Measure the gas line, as you did the water. You can do it either way and include all gas cocks and flex connectors, if needed. And do not forget hangers. Sometimes you may have to look at where you will run the line and figure that out. Other times it is in the drawings. Either way, check the size against the *International Fuel Gas Code.* It may be specified that some of the gas piping be welded above two inches. If so, and you do not have a certified welder, then you will have to hire this out. Be aware that many times you can minimize this by piping longer runs of two inches or less and size them out to provide proper flow to the units. Gas piping will be measured and calculated similar to the other three operations. This is sheet #4.

This project has another system that is a four-inch Victaulic steel line that has a four-inch backflow preventer on it. The purpose of this line is to fill tender trucks in the shop. We will install it. This line will require that all parts and fittings be accounted for, as well as hangers and the backflow preventer. The prints show a six-inch flange at roughly twelve inches above the floor, and that is expressed as AFF for "above finish floor." We will need to reduce to a four-inch line before we can work with this, and we need to change from flanged to Victaulic. The rest of the system will be in Victaulic fittings and couplings, and the pipe is placed as twenty-foot sections. We secured a cut fee from a local agent, so we can cut pipe to the lengths we need and have that done locally in lieu of waiting and ordering this pipe. All water lines will have to be flushed with chlorine, and that is figured into the water line price, with the testing also figured in. All work on the ceiling will require a scissor lift, which we own but should be accounted for in our pricing. If we did not own one, we would have to rent one and may want to rent an additional lift for this project.

Use the local rental fee as your cost structure. This will include a fire department connection fitting, and that is accounted for in this sheet. We kept that as a separate bid sheet due to the size of this portion of the bid. This is sheet #5. This, along with gas piping for this bid, is in the plumbing side of our numbers. There are also four hose reels that were specified. We found a vendor for those, and the water hose reels are in our plumbing price.

This building had an expensive specified exhaust fan system with controls that we are furnishing. While there is little labor for us, there is a large portion of cost, and that was accounted for at the beginning of sheet #6. We secured a bid from the vendor for the specified system and placed that on this sheet. The lower section of this sheet is for the furnace that was specified, which we had to design. So we had some criteria to deal with on the prints, and we created our own list of materials and priced the equipment and on this sheet, as part of our HVAC bid.

Sheet #7 was dedicated to the air piping that was required for this job and also included four hose reels that were specified and from the same vendor as the water hose reels. These, however, were in the HVAC bid, as air lines were specified in that portion of our bid. We used the same procedure for figuring the air lines as we did for the gas and water lines. The air lines are specified as L copper, and we used that price for materials. Do not forget hangers and fittings. You can use the pricing guides if you like or develop your own. For your first few prices it might be a good idea to use a national labor guide to help you envision the labor needed. You may want to use these forever. There are also programs available that will do this for you, and that is an option.

After we prepared these sheets, we then look for items that are specified as an alternate and formulate our pricing for the base bid and alternate bids as directed. We then separated those items out to formulate the base and alternate bids for this project. This is all done on sheet #8, and now we have a final sheet to prepare.

Sheet #9 provides the work space to total all of our materials costs and all labor costs. This is where we put our permit fees. After we have marked up our materials and equipment for our desired profit margin, we add the sales tax on that total, if applicable. If this is for a government entity or a nonprofit, tax is not an issue. Some communities do not levy taxes on materials but collect a use tax when the permit is granted, as part of the fee. That will release us from adding tax to our materials. This will provide the ability to total these prices and create a price we can use as our lump-sum price for this project.

Often we will have to call either the engineer or the owner for clarification on something that is specified. For instance, the specs on this job did not list York as a possible furnace brand that they would accept. Since our pricing on York is better, and that is the brand we normally sell, we wanted to be sure we could use that as our equipment. It would not be profitable to price a York furnace and find out that they would only accept a Carrier. Then we would find our price is 20 percent more for the Carrier. There are few times that you cannot substitute for this type of thing, but it is better to know in advance.

When it comes to bidding on a house with several bathrooms, I normally use a per-fixture price for all plumbing fixtures that includes all labor, and rough-in materials. This is derived by counting all toilets, showers, tubs, lavatories, washers and dryers, and hose bibs, along with the water heater, boiler (if any), and the kitchen sink and all kitchen appliances. Remember that a dishwasher and an ice maker will constitute a fixture for the dishwasher and at least half for the ice maker. A boiler water makeup is figured as a half fixture. I also count floor drains a half fixture unit. After calculating that price, I then create a fixture list, price that out with all trim items, and add labor into that as well. I would keep that as a separate line item, with only your cost plus maybe 10 percent advertised as the fixture allowance. After you are roughed in, if the homeowner wants to furnish all their own fixtures, you can deduct the smaller number only. You do not want to get into providing all the labor to install someone's fixtures for free. Remember that you will still have to provide stops, escutcheons, and supply tubes, and that can run up to thirty dollars per fixture sometimes.

The heating with a furnace in a house like this is similar to the larger jobs. You will have to create a design and do a take-off for ductwork for a price. This is particularly true if you have a larger custom-style house. Options such as cooling, which will have to be priced for each house, and humidifiers and other accessories could be a flat rate charge on a new installation and should always be optioned for on any project. "If you never price an option, you will never sell one."

A boiler system, while there is a myth that you could quote a boiler system at a per-square-foot price, it should be priced out. I have seen some systems with a Triangle Tube boiler that we could do for $4.50 per foot and others that were $7.00, so steer clear of that habit. A range is always good to quote, for sake of conversation, say, $5.00 to $8.00 per foot, reserving the option to actually look at the project and create a real price. Boiler systems are always more expensive than furnaces, with the exception of structural constraints that would have a large effect on the way the ductwork can be installed.

Let's talk about creating value engineering for a project, be it residential or commercial. We installed a large retail space some time ago, which had five rooftop units and was ducted out in the ceiling, about twenty-five feet off the floor. We deleted all ductwork and brought the supply and returns down to a concentric register. We saved about $25,000 on the project. I only deduct the materials at my cost and about 60 percent of the labor we will save when I do that.

Another great example is a car dealer. We deleted the rough top units and installed all Breezeair coolers on this building. This was a large savings but nothing compared to the hot water domestic system that had a central water heater that fed hot water to all over this dealership. It then had to have hot water return lines, or the hot water would have taken fifteen minutes to get to the fixtures. We designed a different concept for hot water and eliminated two lines to each fixture and the main water heater and pump. We saved about $20,000 off the price we had calculated when the prints were drawn. These savings allowed us to create a much better building at a lower cost, and we were heroic and profitable as well—actually more profitable than if we had installed the job at the higher price with the systems designed.

All of this takes a little time and trouble, as you have to establish the cost of the specified building before you can value engineer the changes and strive to never reduce the quality but to enhance it, if at all possible. I have found that it normally is. For some reason, engineers like to stay in the past and design items with which are familiar. If you have a stuck-in-the-mud engineer, you get 1980 technology. That is not as good as you can offer. It is not a situation of a newer version; it is a situation of a lazy designer who does not want to listen to the building owner and possibly is not as educated as their degree would leave you to believe.

I have found that most folks ask for our advice. They may have run into our work somewhere else and seen the value of a little preplanning.

It certainly makes your time spent worth more, and it is satisfying to know you have created a system that is the best you can do at this time.

Always be aware of and open to new technology but not to the extent that you are always trying new stuff just to say you did. Some new items are not that good and will cost you more than you could ever figure. If you have a good boiler brand, for instance, and a salesman wants you to try another high-efficiency model, be aware that they will not be there to make it work, only to deliver the unit and collect the check. Your name is on the job and will affect your relationship as you go into the future. You do not want to have to live that one down. Use what you know about equipment. And if the supplier is not trustworthy, do not buy from them.

At one time there was a sales rep for a brand of furnace that many people sell who came into my shop and was wearing plaid polyester pants. He tried to get me to try several products, and then he exclaimed, "Come on, man! You got to give me a chance." You can imagine that I told him in a very polite tone where he could go and also where to put his equipment that I did not like and showed him the door. Sell you and your brand, not some other brand that a manufacturer or sales rep wants you to.

Many times we are presented with a project that has been drawn and specified and comes in at a higher price for the entire building than the owner wants to spend. They still want the building, and they still want to spend a large amount of money, but they do not want to spend as much as the prints will require. This is due to not having any construction folks in play at the time of meetings with the designer. You will get to the point that you help design buildings, as the owner may be a longtime customer and trust your judgment. Never take that lightly. You have much greater flexibility with the project than if you are bound by a set of drawings and a mechanical engineer's designs. I have seen many prints of late that call out that the mechanical contractor designed small systems, as the owner did not want to spend the money for an engineer and hired an architect to create the drawings for them. A few have called for our opinion, and others think they know it all. The know-it-alls are usually ripe for value engineering.

The term "value engineering" (or VE, as many call it) comes with a set of horrors. Often it means the mechanical and bones of the building are the systems that are compromised rather than carpet and trim which is easy to update later. That being said, if you approach this with the idea of reducing costs without compromising quality, you usually are the winner.

I mentioned earlier that you always have to start with what is drawn and specified. I have rarely been beaten on a job when someone comes in with a low price. We look at the fact that they did not bid per the plans and specs. I can remember only one time in twenty-seven years that this happened. I have found that when we are given the opportunity to price the job with the same materials or specifications, we usually come out on top of that project.

Let's use the idea of a metal building or any commercial building, for instance, that is specified with L copper and insulation, with all water piping installed overhead. The materials and labor factor comes at a high cost. Most of the time there are only a few fixtures included in this project. The reason for this is a mind-set that having the pipe accessible is a better idea. In the past, before PEX and the use of it under a slab with some foam insulation and no joints under the slab, that may have been a true concept. Today, with PEX coming in five-hundred-foot rolls and the idea of placing this under the concrete floor, I am comfortable with underground water piping for this use and using a manifold concept to serve the fixtures as a group. Normally the water piping can be installed in one to two days with a materials cost of around 30–50 percent of the other method of piping. Depending on the size of the building, you may take a week of labor to install and insulate the line. If it is cold only, the insulation is for condensation only.

I have seen copper fail, but never PEX, unless it has been frozen hard. Copper will not take the freeze that PEX will, so I am comfortable that this is a good solution for this VE concept. So now let's talk about pricing this change. I normally take out my cost of the beginning materials only, reduce the labor to reflect that savings, and then add back in my new cost of materials for this change. Most of the time, if you can show a deduction of 30 percent, you are a hero. On a national average, plumbing and HVAC are normally 15–25 percent of any project cost, so you cannot save the entire project by yourself.

If you can reduce all portions of a project by 20 percent, then a project that was originally estimated at $1 million on can be saved. I am sure the client will find the building very comfortable and serviceable if VE is approached and quality is maintained while reducing costs. This concept will never have a serviceable effect on this building but will save possibly thousands of dollars in installation costs.

I reduce my price but raise my profit margin every time I value engineer one of these projects. This, of course, should remain our little secret, though I have shared it with some good customers. They are usually happy that they spent less and I made more. I might buy a new truck with the profit on a dealership building, as I did with the project described in the earlier part of this chapter.

I have seen restaurants still specifying cast-iron waste and drain. I always change that, not for a price factor but for serviceability. PVC waste and drain under the slab installed in a restaurant will always work better than cast iron, and under-the-slab fire rating is not a concern.

Several years ago we were asked to price a heated makeup air system for a commercial kitchen hood. You can buy a nice system that includes an evaporative cooling section and all the bells and whistles for an installed price of $15,000. The equipment may cost you $8,000. You can install a good side discharge evaporative cooler with an outdoor rated duct heater that has a stainless steel heat exchanger and build your own skid for far less, with an equipment cost of 25–35 percent of the makeup air unit. It will do the same things and usually provide better cooling and reduce the installed cost by about 65–75 percent of the prices I used for an example. I have many of these around our area, and all have worked very well. You can even place an indoor duct heater under a roof-mounted cooler, and that works very well. I always use a single inlet cell deck cooler or a roof-mounted cell deck cooler, and I always use a power-vented duct heater. These should not present the problem of venting combustion products with this type of system. The entire system can be controlled with a simple cooler switch, or you can get as fancy as you like. A simple light switch will start the duct heater in the winter, with the duct stat controlling the output temperature.

These examples come from years of experience and a belief that an open and prepared mind can create solutions that no competitor can or will. Learn the products you can offer, and always look at how to do the job with the highest quality and the lowest cost to you. Any installation that works, performs at a high comfort standard, is safe, and passes code is a great one, no matter what the cost. And there is more than one way to skin a cat.

A recent quote about our efforts came from a very good architect when he asked a general contractor why they always spend big dollars on engineers and have to hire us to make it work no matter who installed it. I hope to place it on my gravestone. What more could you say about someone in their pursuit of excellence in their trade?

Currently we are doing a custom home in Wyoming with this architect. He did not hire a mechanical engineer to design the ductwork and heating. This job is so large that we are there on a time and materials basis, as the one and a half hours of drive time each way hamper our ability to price this job accurately.

As you progress in this business, remember that a bid opening is a simple poker game, where the low hand wins. It is imperative for your survival to hone your skills and be sure that you have covered your bases when you submit a bid, as you can either make a great profit or suffer a huge loss. The management of the project is also important, as you do not have the freedom to make the costly mistakes that some employees make, such as time and the choice of installation techniques and materials used. It should come as no surprise that a hard dollar bid is just that. Even if you figured it correctly, you can find yourself a loser if you do not watch the project for progress and proper materials.

There are times when a tech will install what they think is best and not hold the interest of the company at heart. This is usually caused by not being trained and appreciated. Also discipline is imperative, as you may never change some leopard's spots. If you find they can never make you a profit, then you need to make a change.

There will also be the individuals who have your back. Do not be afraid to appreciate and reward them, as they will only serve to strengthen your company in ways you may never be able to see.

Changing Courses

We have discussed the concepts that you may use or have used to start your business, and now we will discuss what happens when, for one reason or another, you want to make a course change. Let's say you are an HVAC forced air contractor and want to add hydronics and refrigeration to your toolbox. These same ideas can be used for any time you want to grow your offerings. Never let yourself say, "If I do not offer this, someone else will." These words are the introduction to failure. I have watched many people say this as they embarked on their last endeavor in business. Never let yourself be drawn into a field or product offering that you have not vetted as a profit center for your business or as one that you have not made the plan to help you succeed in this offering.

Businesses often take on new offerings in an attempt to remain relevant in the industry they serve. Never let yourself get to the point that your actions are driven by areas of the market you have not fully investigated.

When I began my career in plumbing/HVAC, I entered as a master plumber who had worked in industrial piping and was also well versed in temperature controls. The skills I had as a young technician were ample to understand the controls of any furnace at the time and also to solve any plumbing or heating problem with which I was presented. I was also very well versed in hydronic heating. At that time that meant a boiler and baseboard heaters to convey the BTUs needed to heat the space. I was not a sheet metal worker, though I had worked for combination shops early on and understood what the tools did. Service work was the available option and was also the only real source of work in our area at the time. However, I longed to install new systems, as that was a big part of my background. I set out to build a business based on what I knew and what I wanted to do. There will be times when the market dictates what you do, even if it is not really your cup of tea.

As I grew, I subcontracted to a one-man sheet metal shop to provide those services, and we installed many large jobs. It was not the most profitable time, as the cost for the sheet metal work was more due to the nature of using a subcontractor for that work. We even rented a shop together, and we were able to dissolve amicably when he wanted to move and I did not want to. I took that opportunity to buy my own equipment and hire my own sheet metal worker.

I believe that all mechanical contractors should perform both plumbing and HVAC and that refrigeration is a possible service to leave out, but that is not a rule anywhere, so you can choose what you want to do. The diversification of offering several different types of work has been good for me, but you may not want that, and your market may dictate you are not needed in one of the divisions I mentioned. The market in which we operate needs us to do it, while forty miles away we are needed mostly for sheet metal and HVAC.

Let's discuss changing courses. Let's say that, at this time, you are an HVAC contractor who is thinking about hydronic heat as an option. This is in your mind as you look at plumbing contractors doing this type of heat, and you have to service the boiler. Many plumbers can install pipes, but few are good at troubleshooting control problems. For this change in course, you will have to learn a few new things about how to convey the BTUs with hydronic heat. This will be easier than learning about forced air and the different things needed for that.

Let's ask questions about why you want to open this new frontier to your business. I presume that you plan to install quality systems at an affordable and profitable price and provide the same level of service and expertise you exhibit in your HVAC offerings.

1. Are you getting numerous calls to install or maintain hydronic systems? Are they from good and trusted customers?
2. Have you tried some systems?
3. Do you understand how to price these for profit?
4. Do you have a supplier to help with this transition?
5. Does your staff want to learn a new technology, or will you have to hire?
6. What is your competition in this area? Are they competent? Have they made the market unprofitable?
7. Do you want to install all types of hydronic or only radiant floor or only baseboard?
8. Is snow melt a need or an option to your business?
9. Do you want to look at large boiler systems in large commercial spaces?
10. Are you well versed in different piping arrangements and installation techniques?
11. Will this require more equipment to make this change?

Answering these questions will make the decision easier. This concept can be used for any change, even the decision to remove a service from your offerings. The questions above will be addressed with the intention to be a top-notch contractor for these services. Many have tried to break into a field that they know nothing about, thinking that they can be successful in that field without instruction, experience, or help. They tend to do a disservice to the clients who use them and foul up the market for all involved, leaving a bad name for the good contractors and for the systems as a whole.

Question 1: Are you getting calls, and from whom? Many times I have witnessed contractors who decide they are getting "a lot of calls" to perform a new service. In some minds that is two to three calls. In my mind it should be twenty to thirty before I determine that there is a need for my investment. Monitor the quality of these calls. Are they folks like one I had, who wanted me to drive a hundred miles one way to work on his boiler in his apartment complex, when there was a very competent friend of mine who operated in that small town? Upon investigation I discovered that he would not pay his bills, and this guy had shut him off. Why would I drive two hundred miles round trip and not get paid? Sometimes you will get these calls from committed and good customers, and they bear more weight on my decision than someone I do not know. Many contractors have gone broke chasing something they deem as a real profit maker, only to find there was not any profit there, and they eventually lost their business while seeking quick fortune.

Question 2: Have you tried one of these systems? Often we jump into a job thinking we understand what the needs are. If you have tried a hydronic system or any other system, you will have a greater understanding of how this may provide profit and workload to your business. Never just look at another contractor who is very successful in a field and think it is simple to provide these services. All work done well will present issues that you need to be aware of. If you do not become aware of these, you will be sorry, or you will do the customer and yourself a major disservice. Early on I dealt with a Roto-Rooter dealer who told me that he did not want to work on boilers and would send those jobs to me. After he decided he could solder copper and do boiler change-outs as my competitor, and I had to save his bacon on about four systems, I refused to help again. I let him know that if he wanted to be in the boiler business, he should get the training to do it and not depend on my help any longer. If you tried one and were happy with the results, then that is one vote for the change in business model.

Question 3: Do you understand how to price these for profit? Each new endeavor will contain some details that you may not know or understand. Have you surveyed your costs, the market, and the number of systems you might be able to add to your workload? What will the labor cost be for this new adventure? How about new special equipment? What are current competitors charging, and will that provide you the profit and the ability to perform at the level you want? Are there enough customers to warrant your change in direction? All of these questions need to be answered to make a decision about this new endeavor.

Question 4: Do you have a supplier who can help? If you are a forced air contractor, you may be tempted to buy boilers and equipment from the supplier with whom you are dealing. Be aware that they may know less about boilers than the hydronic and plumbing houses do about forced air. I have found most reputable suppliers will help if you show that you will progress into a premier contractor. If you do not, they are usually unwilling to help you further. I recommend a partnership with a reputable supplier for hydronic heating. Do not rely on a supplier who is adding this to their business in a half-hearted way. They will do the same thing for the supply side of the market. Several years ago I had a plumbing supplier who began to sell WeatherKing, which is a good brand of equipment. At the time, all furnaces I bought were shipped to me, and I paid freight. This supplier decided to provide freight-free delivery, and I bought from him for a while. It became clear that, to resolve all the problems they were having, they called me, as I knew forced air and was the only one to whom they were selling who did. All the rest were plumbers without my background. I had to inform them that if I was to spend several hours on the phone with them, diagnosing problems, I needed to be paid. They decided they were really not equipped to sell forced air. It was better for all concerned.

Question 5: Does your staff want to learn? If your staff is not engaged, and they do not want to better themselves, you will struggle to make this change unless you staff up for it. These types of problems may signal bigger problems than just a change in where you are going. If your staff does not want the challenge, it will make your challenge much larger. If you happen to be lucky enough to have a great hydronic tech fall into your lap, then the challenge may be less problematic.

Question 6: Is your competition competent? There are times when you are faced with a competitor who is not in your field, and you are not in theirs, and both of you are very competent. I normally would not want to go up against them, as they already have a good handle on the market and how to operate in it. The other part of this is how they are pricing the work. Will you only get the calls for the price seekers? That will make your entry into the field more difficult and should be given some thought. A longtime competent contractor will usually have learned how to price the work, or they would not still be there. If they were far too high, they would not get any work. If they were too low, they would have gone bankrupt. There are markets, however, to which you may be the catalyst for change. You can make good money while you grow and add business to your load. Sometimes you will be faced with a contractor who is willing to work as a one-man shop for the wages he would make working for you. That individual will always bring the market down and price his work way lower than you would. Remember that he sees the labor rate as all his money and total profit, and you see it as part of your profit. I have seen contractors price jobs for my cost plus as little as $500 for their labor. To them, they are making $500; to me, they are losing $1,200 or more. You will look like the thief to that client, and that will mean you will not get the job. Be thankful for that, as it is not a winning situation.

Question 7: What type of hydronic will you install? The answer to this is driven by four options: your desire, your skills, your market, and your climate. Hydronic heat will work anywhere in the world that heat is needed, so let's talk about desire first. Let's say you want to do high-end mansions in your market, and there is a need for radiant floor heat. That will dictate that you master radiant floor. Do you have the skills for this? Let's assume you do and that you are ready to take off into this field. What is your market like? Do you live in an area that does not have high-end housing or many commercial boiler options? This may dictate what type of hydronic work you do. Finally, what is your climate like? Here in the mountains we install not only radiant floor but snow melt as well. Once you have the reputation as an expert, the world is your oyster. We have installed many systems, and some of those have been $100,000 and more. The per-square-foot price is twice what some quote, but ours work and use less fuel than others. We have developed a market for this type of work, and we are awarded many difficult projects, with no other bidders in the mix. The same can be said for boiler change-outs. We can produce great profit from this work as well. Baseboard is beginning to be a real option again—not the old type we all see but very decorative systems, and those command the same pricing as radiant floor.

Question 8: Will you do snow melt? That will be determined by your climate. While we install a lot of it in the mountains, it is not very prevalent in lower elevations, as the snow is not as great there. Many parts of the north and the mountain region see it a lot. As I mentioned earlier, it can be very profitable.

Question 9: Do you want to look at large commercial boiler systems? These can again become a specialist market for you, as many contractors will do only small residential systems, and these tend to command a higher price and, if the work is completed correctly, a greater customer loyalty.

Question 10: Are you well versed in piping? Can you thread pipe? Can you weld pipe? Can you solder large-diameter copper? All of these are needed to install larger boilers and, to some extent, even smaller boilers. If all you have ever soldered is 7/8-inch copper, you need to become comfortable with two-inch to four-inch copper, depending on the systems you may install. The worst thing you can do is have multiple leaks on large-diameter copper and not discover it until the system is purged and charged with heating glycol. What a mess, and what a profit destroyer.

Question 11: Will you need more equipment? All new endeavors will need some new equipment, and you will have to buy that with the profits from your other areas of business. While we have used a move to hydronic heat as our example, the move from plumbing to forced air will require a larger investment and one that you must account for. All of us understand small tools and trucks, but the idea of now having a sheet metal shop may be difficult to swallow. All changes in direction will present some costs. If we count those and price accordingly, we can become profitable in any area with the questions answered. Of course, there will be other questions that may be unique to your situation, but with these eleven questions we can usually determine if we should embark into a new branch of our business or not.

What happens when you decide you have invested in an area that is not profitable, and it is time to quit? I worked for a company in Denver many years ago, before I went into business, and I referenced this employer in another chapter. He is the one who told me I had the stuff and encouraged me to get in and stay in. He changed his total business two times that I know of. When I worked for him I ran the last construction project that he did, and that was in 1984. After bidding and hiring individuals to get into that market, they decided they should go back to just doing the large commercial service work for which they were built. This company was started by my employer as a branch of a large mechanical contractor who needed a service department to handle the warranty period from the large schools, hospitals, and other large projects they were doing. They set up this business, and my employer and his partner bought it from them sometime later. The business did large service contracts for commercial and industrial buildings all over the front range of Colorado. I did the last construction project at that time, and while I was told that my job had actually made a profit, they realized that this was not for them, and they were leaving this market after the completion of my project.

A few years later, I went to visit my former employer, who had again changed the whole business model. Now they were doing residential and light commercial and left the heavy commercial customers for a much larger profit. A total transformation took place, and at the time I was there to visit, they were installing two to three furnace and AC systems per day all over their area.

What a gutsy move, changing their operation in the course of just eight years and totally transforming from what they started as to what they were now. Most of us would not be so bold and probably not be as profitable either.

At one time I did not only plumbing but drain line cleaning as well. As soon as I could, I sold that machine for a loss—not because I did not see a market for the service, but because I did not like to do that. There was a time when I sold the refrigeration portion of my business to an employee so he could, in his words, "make big money fast," like I did. He lasted for only a couple of years, and I spent the money he gave me and started with a new refrigeration tech and went back into that work.

I have made some of those changes in the past. While I told you that I am a plumber by trade, we now do as much (or more) forced air HVAC each year as we do plumbing. Some years we do very little new installation plumbing. We always have a profit center there, but it has been some time since we have grossed more in plumbing than HVAC and hydronic heating.

Your direction can change (and should) if there is a profitable and enjoyable reason to do so. I spoke with a young plumber at a conference, and he had the opportunity to purchase a one-man sheet metal shop in his area that had a good reputation. The former owner would work for him for a while. I first thought about whether he should do this. Then I wanted to make him understand that he needed to get out of the truck, begin to run the business, and not continue to do service calls all day every day. I cannot tell you the outcome of that discussion, but at that time in my life I would have applied these questions and valued the purchase with the answers. I think I would have bought the company and not gone through the growing I did to establish my company, but I did not have that opportunity.

Change for the sake of change is something we all do from time to time, but change to improve yourself can be profitable if you have the diligence to evaluate the outcome and find the risk worth the reward. Or, as I have asked before, is the juice worth the squeeze?

Community Involvement and Helpful Relationships

One of the most rewarding things I have ever experienced is being available to help with the growth or issues in our community. There are several ways of doing this, and I will attempt to outline them with multiple illustrations of my experience in this arena.

The bible refers to the need for us to help widows and fatherless children. As a mechanical contractor, I have had many experiences that were from this part of community involvement. I received a call to fix a gas cooktop for an elderly woman who had received a nice used cooktop, but it was not operational. She was on a very meager fixed income, and I decided that we could install this if she just paid for the parts I used. It was my labor anyway, and if I wanted to give it away I could. I needed a carpenter, so I enlisted a general contractor and told him what we were doing. He agreed, although he was not well versed in the concept of helping the widows and fatherless.

We went to her house, and he cut the countertop for me while I ran the gas to the area and installed the gas cock and a flex. We set this cooktop into place and fired it up. This was an old house, and it was very apparent that this lady did not have much to provide for herself. We hooked it up, and she was delighted. We jumped into our truck, and my carpenter said, "What did you say we were doing?" I repeated the phrase, and his response was "That felt really good." Not only did we meet the need of this lady, but my carpenter friend was schooled in the joy of helping someone who needed the help but could not afford to pay. Together we have installed several projects like this since then. This was not a front-page news item, as I am sure only the lady, the carpenter, and I knew about it (until now). I do not tell this for any other reason than to drive home the fact that we have been given much, and as an industry we should be good stewards of that reward. I also believe that it is paid back with very generous interest as we move forward.

Once you are able to operate a mechanical contracting business, you have reached a business mind-set. You have the ability to be one of the better businesspeople in your community. Embrace that, and use your talents to move your community forward whenever you can. Be a guiding light in your community. There is not a financial indicator to which you can trace this, and you cannot track an increase in traffic to your business, as folks rarely say, "We are using you because you did this for our community." However, it will pay back dividends in your life and your business as you move forward.

Never be afraid to leverage the resources you have to help on a worthy community project or to help someone in need. You have to decide what that means for you and your operation. I tend to help with things that reach out to children. However, I will not sponsor baseball, as I really do not like that sport. I sponsor football, hockey, basketball, rodeo, track, soccer, and even some skiing. I also am involved financially in Young Life and our local Boys and Girls Club, as a donor and a board member. This has been very rewarding for me personally, and I highly recommend it. I also have coached youth football for several years, and the young folks I have had a chance to engage have been a total joy. Being in this business has been very rewarding in what it has allowed me to do with my extra time, resources, and dollars.

We have helped our local hockey rink by donating plumbing work and helping to fulfill other building needs. The greatest joy you will ever experience is in helping others who appreciate and deserve that help. I find that there is never a risk to doing this, only pure rewards.

I am asked many times by other businesspeople to look at what they are doing and how they might improve their business. That is another way you can help. But always remember that you must find someone who can be a sounding board for you. Iron sharpens iron, and we all need that interaction with folks whom we can believe in and look up to.

Take each opportunity to learn as many things as you can from others, and you will be amazed at the degree in life this gives you.

I was talking to the manager of the city's road and bridge department, and we got onto the subject of trucks and fleet management. He was surprised when I told him that I had learned how to manage my fleet while watching him during my time on the city council. He is very good at knowing when to keep a truck and when to trade a truck, and I found that the city's fleet was well managed and had little downtime. No HVAC trade school will teach you that. While there are those who want to do this for you, it is because they can profit from your ignorance. You can learn how to do this yourself. I was lucky to find someone to imitate in a town of fifteen thousand people. He never realized I did that until I told him some ten years after I was no longer on the council.

When we talk about those who sharpened me, I have to give credit to three. The first is a man who moved to Grand Junction and started an HVAC supply company that later became a Johnstone. Bill Olsen was a man who had been in the sheet metal trade and supply business for years and was always available to give me little insights into business and things I should look for. He commanded respect and was always there as a friend and a mentor. We went on trips with him and attended the Chicago ASHRAE trade shows with him. He was the first to say, "If you never quote a humidifier, you will never sell one." That opened my eyes to thinking out of the box. My love and respect for him was so deep that I was willing to give away tickets to a Denver Broncos playoff game to attend his funeral.

The training and encouragement I have received from National Comfort Institute have been instrumental in my life. The people who work there deserve credit. From the first air balance class I took from Rob Falke to each time I am with the other members, I find these moments to be invaluable to me and to my company and to the culture I have always desired to achieve. Being a lone wolf is a very stressful and lonely experience, but with NCI I never feel alone. This group of contractors are like a band of brothers who help me in a time of need with ideas and encouragement. I am amazed at the celebration of success we enjoy at every summit I have attended. Sometimes I think about how Bill would have enjoyed this group and what he could have brought to the table.

The third man is Pres Askew, who was very instrumental in my involvement with the Boys and Girls Club. While I served as mayor and on the city council, Pres and his wife, Patty, moved to Craig from Denver to be close to their grandchildren. It was a blessing for this community. They built a new home that we were contracted to plumb and heat. Then Pres decided I needed mentoring, and we met for breakfast many times. The morning he outlined the concept and need of the club was eye-opening, as he painted a picture of the great things we could do. Then he dropped the bomb that we only needed to raise $400,000 per year to do this. My feeble brain at the time could not conceive that, as we could barely maintain $50,000 to have a Young Life part-time director. He taught me that money is not the problem; focus is the problem.

We now have a budget of $1 million for the Club. We are in both Craig and Steamboat Springs, and it is the fifth largest Club in Colorado. Pres also had been in the financial service industry and was responsible for keeping his employees producing. He always said that if you think it is time to make a personnel change, it was probably time six months ago. He taught me to hire slow and fire fast. I served with him on the board of the Club, and he gave each of us a copy of *Good to Great,* which transformed my thinking as to how I should view my company. What a watershed event this has been in my life.

You may come from an environment that has led you to believe that you can be on your own and you need no other help to survive. You are the master of your destiny, and that is the reason that you wanted to be in business in the first place. You do not need others to tell you what to do. The fallacy of that is now everyone tells you what to do. Being in business only increases your boss quotient, as now every customer (and even at times your employees) will attempt to tell you what to do. The customers who call and complain or demand are now your boss. The employee who, in the spur of the moment, tells you that he is taking next week off because it is spring break and he deserves that is now your boss. You have entered an arena that is not what you thought it was. The sooner you realize and accept that, the sooner you will begin to thrive and profit from your decisions.

Mankind was not designed to live alone, with no companionship. That is spelled out in the book of Genesis. The sooner you build relationships that will hold you up in times of need and allow you to share others' burdens in times of prosperity, the better off you will be. While you will think that you can continue on your own, you need to be able to share, be challenged, participate, and build relationships with others in similar situations—those who will understand where you are and what you are doing. This cannot be your favorite employee but should be someone in a business or with some management in their background. Iron really sharpens iron, and the more you seek this type of relationship, the sooner you will be sharp.

Let's talk about your recreational time and what you do outside of your business. I have watched for years as different individuals went into business to have more free time. However, if you are in business to succeed, you will have less free time for several years, and that will be the thing you invest to reap the rewards later. If you are looking to embark because you see your employer going on great trips and having all the money you think he wants, then think again. Your personal wealth and assets are now the property of the business, and you are the sole employee who is responsible for its care and feeding. I am not saying that it is not rewarding in the least. However, I am addressing the thought that being in business is a license to take multiple vacations or hunting trips or do any other activity you find relaxing and fun. I know of several here in the "Elk Hunting Capital of the World" who think hunting season is a two- to three-month event, and if there is work to be done, it will have to wait. Since I do not hunt, I was able to profit from their lack of dedication. If you look at your boss and think, *Boy, he has it made,* you should drive by the office on Saturday and Sunday and see if his truck is there. You do not have to go to the office every weekend, but you will go at times.

John was a young general contractor and had a successful business. He was considered by many to be the up-and-coming front-runner for the next great contractor in our area. His talent and commitment to excellence were admirable for a young man of less than forty. Two employees who had worked for him for several years decided they could do better for themselves and resigned with little notice and spread the rumor to their friends that John was not a good boss. He was obviously hit in the gut by this development and told me, "I don't know why I do this. I am just going to get a job and forget this stuff." John has taken more vacations with his family than most guys in our area do. He did not hunt, but he took multiple trips with the kids and wife at spring break and other times of the year. At the same time, this business was adding to his personal wealth in the form of rental properties and other sources of residual income.

The employees, by the way, did not secure general contractor licenses for some time. I had to remind John that he had taken more trips in his short business career than I had taken in twenty-seven years, and he really was now finding out some of the pitfalls. He was not built to be an employee and would have less free time to pursue his other interests or take trips. I reminded him that if he worked for me, I would expect him at work five days a week for at least forty-nine weeks per year, and he would not have the freedom to leave at the drop of the hat, like he was accustomed to. He decided to man up and go back to work, providing a job for new guys. He now has included Sheetrock in his business, which he had always subcontracted. I am not saying that this was not a difficult road, but the actual difficult time was short-lived, and he is now able to build back up with a new course and concentrate on getting back to where he felt he was. It is my experience that any time an employee leaves like this, I become more profitable, as I was not seeing the true picture of their dedication and productivity but was living in a fantasy land of what I perceived they were to the company.

My son, Troy, owned a graphic design and sign business in our small community. He was contacted by a local tourism director to create a brochure to pass out during a large statewide bicycle event. He gave them a price, and they agreed. The director was known to not take care of business, and Troy told her that she had to have the information for design to him no less than two weeks before the event to allow for design, printing, and delivery. The information was slow to come, even with his prompting.

About four days before the event, the director brought in the information. Troy's first reaction was "I am screwed. I cannot do this." After a brief mental reorganization from dear old Dad, he realized that, no, he could not do that for the quoted price. Could he deliver at any price? A call to the printer to request a quick print price and one late night spent in front of the computer might allow him to deliver the product. He called the director and explained that, due to the delayed information, he would have to quick-print this project, and the cost would rise. He was given the okay to proceed. Before the event, the brochures were ready to be picked up, still hot from the press. He profited much more than planned. What did it cost? One late night doing design on a computer, which is what he loves to do anyway, and the attitude to deliver the product and not "just say no" because they did not follow his ideas. That director is no longer with the tourism group, and Troy was not the goat that did not perform but the hero who came through.

You should put the business third in line, behind God and your family, but never use them as an excuse for your own lazy and slothful attitude. You and your business will not profit from that, and you'll end up making more as an employee for a profitable firm. Then you can go home at night and not think about anything but yourself. It is my belief, which is based on many years of observation, that you can make good money and prepare your life and give to things you hold dear if you approach this business as a leader. If you don't, you will make more money as an employee of someone who does.

I am constantly confronted by individuals who think that they are building a business to close and be gone in three to five years. That type of business is only there for complete profit and pillaging. Eventually that will catch up to you. As you go through life as a contractor, you will meet hundreds of individuals who used to be in business for themselves. Have you ever wondered why they are no longer in business for themselves? In the course of life, just like the two young employees of the general contractor I spoke of, you will meet many who think they have the stuff to do this on their own. I never discount those who have the ability to do so. However, there will always be a group of folks who have been in and out of business several times. There will also be those that start a business and have no ethics. What they will do to your industry is criminal and leads to the jokes about what we charge. I am not saying that the laborer is not worth his hire, but you will encounter competitors and fly-by-night contractors who come to town and take advantage of many folks. While they will always exist, make sure that you do not develop an attitude that will be harmful for your future. You will find that they come and go and really do not impact you as much as you think they might.

Most problems that develop in your business will be from another problem that was allowed to fester and infect all around (both employees and customers), and they are usually internal. Sometimes it starts with the head of the organization and goes down through the ranks, and other times it is how we deal with outside threats and competition that makes the problem loom larger. Since we are talking about relationships, I will address those with competitors and other contractors.

When I started my journey, a friend told me that I made another contractor nervous more than any other individual who had begun to do business in our small town. Later I found this second-generation contractor, who was one of the oldest Lennox dealers in the United States. He was not a bad guy, and I had a good relationship with him. We allowed each other to take parts and then replace them from our inventories, if needed. That is remarkable, and the actual relationship became clear when we moved to the location in 1996 (which we still use).

Remember that the reputation you build can be yours, or you can take a good one and either make it better or ruin it. A good name is better than riches, and that is up to you.

Relationships with Contractors and Suppliers

It seems to me that we should touch on business relationships that you will encounter as you go along this journey. The first will be that with your suppliers. It does not matter if you want to only do service work or total contracting. You will need suppliers and maybe subcontractors who not only are a means of making your work progress but also have your interests at heart.

Over the years I have initiated and terminated supplier and subcontractor relationships when the situation dictated we do so. For the most part, I have purchased all our HVAC and control items from the same company in Grand Junction for twenty-seven years. They have been not only a supplier but a friend and mentor to us. When a problem comes up, they know that we spend a lot of money with them, and they desire to service our account and meet our expectations. Many suppliers are only there for the sale today and not for the service tomorrow. This group not only sells us furnaces but also repairs parts and attempts to stock a lot of inventory that the normal HVAC warehouse does not. "We can get that from the factory" is a common comment.

While for HVAC I have tied us to one supplier for the most part, on the plumbing side of our business I have had three or four who were our first choice. Right now we enjoy a good relationship with one in Steamboat Springs, about forty miles from us. This will not change if you are in a large city. There will still be those who believe they need to sell boilers and plumbing fixtures and never have the parts you need. When a problem comes up, you might as well have bought that stuff on eBay. I view our subcontractors in the same light as our suppliers. From time to time I have had to contract with electricians and crane operators. The ones we use are always there for us, and that is a two-way street.

Let's say that your supplier has a real problem with a boiler or furnace. They cannot figure it out and call you to do so. Be assured that your time will be paid for, but also be aware that helping them will go a long way, as they have helped you. The same is true for an electrician who we use. If he were to call, I would feel obliged to help him out with a problem that I could address, as he has helped me with mine. You will not create these relationships by always having it your way. There are times you may have to give a little, but compromise is one of the strengths on which our nation was built. Often I have worked on a furnace or boiler that another contractor installed for someone and did not take care of the situation, so the supplier was called. Not only did I help a friend (and someone who has helped me), but I also gained a customer when I was the hero of the situation.

I look forward to seeing our suppliers and subcontractors. I cherish our relationship. But as I said, I have changed main plumbing suppliers several times because I was not being served. I found someone who wanted to help me with my business because I helped their business by being a customer. That type of relationship creates great respect and mutually beneficial situations that money cannot buy. We could not put a price on if it could.

I have had a relationship with general contractors for many years, and that comes from always doing their work and also having their best interests at heart. If you install new construction, you will meet general contractors who do not value you as a subcontractor and only want to find the least-expensive price. I recommend steering clear of them, as they are not profitable in the long run. They will demand more and expect you to make less than general contractors make. Over the years I have found many who are great to work with, and I've kept those. And I have actively decided to terminate my relationship with the ones who are not.

When dealing with a general contractor, you have to provide a service to them that justifies your price. When you do, they should be mindful that you want to make a profit, and if you do not profit, they probably will not either. We just completed a poorly run project that had minimal organization, and the general contractor did not take any responsibility for his lack of management. Everything was someone else's fault, and the project showed that. I am used to having a timeline for completion, having the items, and answering questions in a timely manner in order to proceed. That did not happen. I will never work for this guy again, but the owner of the property wants us to work on another project for him. I've told you of the gut feeling I get, and this is one I ignored because of my previous relationship with the owner. I really wished I had refused the project, as that would have damaged our relationship less than working on this horrible project, which, in theory, should have been an easy and profitable one.

I also have great relationships with general contractors who are concerned not only with themselves but with the subcontractors who they hire as well. If you perform for them, they will sell work and manage work for you so you can thrive. If you do not perform, they will find another subcontractor to take your place. The relationship will slowly develop as you both try to do good work and make a profit while doing so.

Garner good suppliers and general contractors, like you would a good customer, and your life will be much richer in the long run. We consider our local Chevrolet dealer to be a partner in our business, as he takes care of our trucks, sells us new ones, and uses us for all his mechanical needs. I've considered him a supplier for twenty-seven years as well. We perform service work for him, and I sit on a bank board with him. We also have plumbed and heated his new house and his new dealership in Steamboat Springs. In the years I have dealt with him, I have only bought one car from another dealer. That was my new Corvette, and he arranged the deal with a friend of his in Fort Collins. Not only did I get a deal equal to internet pricing, but this dealer took my personal check because of our relationship. Needless to say, I compensated this dealer with a free service and new pads for his Breezeair evaporative cooler at his house. He worked harder on this deal than for any vehicle I had ever purchased from him. It was not for the reward or profit; it was to help me fulfill my dream of a new blue Jetstream Corvette. That is above and beyond, and my life is richer because of our relationship.

I made this chapter the last you read on purpose, as I know that the other things we talked about will reward your life if you have the stuff and you follow the desires of your heart. The other ideas are nothing more than personal situations I have lived through. I shared them to hopefully help you to navigate through or avoid them all. I am convinced that if you take even one small nugget of truth from any of these chapters, this will be your destination. It would not be right (dare I say, it would be a sin) if I did not admonish you to think about the community that blessed you in your business endeavors. While the other chapters may help to increase your bank account, this one will increase your soul. It is a reward far richer than money, fame, or any other thing our society chases today.

Good luck to you in all you do. If after reading this you decide this business is not for you, then I believe it was worth my time to jot down my thoughts. If after reading this you decide it is for you and in some way this has helped, then the juice really was worth the squeeze.

If you are already in business and find some encouragement and make some changes, then my time has really been worth the effort and the juice just paid off in multiples of the squeeze.

Good luck, and Godspeed.

www.ingramcontent.com/pod-product-compliance
Lightning Source LLC
Chambersburg PA
CBHW030802180526
45163CB00003B/1129